LOOKING FOR PEACE? TRY CONFESSION!

By Mary Ann Budnik

R.B. Media, INC.

Springfield, IL

IMPRIMATUR: Reverend Monsignor Richard F. Stika, V.G.
Vicar General of the Archdiocese of St. Louis, MO
Nihil Obstat: Reverend John Jay Hughes
Archdiocese of St. Louis
March 25, 1997

The Nihil Obstat and Imprimatur are a declaration that a book or pamphlet is considered to be free from doctrinal or moral error.

The publisher does not endorse the claims of any purported visionary and recognizes and accepts that the final authority regarding all claimed apparitions within the Catholic Church rests with the Holy See of Rome, to whose judgment we willingly submit.

First Printing: July 16, 1997
Second Printing: March 25, 1998
Third Printing: May 1, 2000

For additional copies of *Looking for Peace? Try Confession!* ($11.95 plus $4.00 for Priority Mail) or for Mary Ann Budnik's first book, *You Can Become a Saint!* ($13.95 plus $4.00 for Priority Mail), individuals, bookstores and book distributors should contact:
R. B. Media, Inc.

14064 Monterey Estates Drive
Delray Beach, FL. 33446
Phone (561) 498-5922
Website: www.rbmediainc.com
E-Mail: mabudnik@comcast.net

Library of Congress Card Number: 00-190498

ISBN 0-9700021-2-2

Table of Contents

ACKNOWLEDGMENTS v

DEDICATION vii

INTRODUCTION ix

CHAPTER 1
   The Necessity Of Confession 1

CHAPTER 2
   How Intensely God Loves You! 13

CHAPTER 3
   Reconciliation Is A Priceless Gift From God 25

CHAPTER 4
   Look Carefully Then How You Walk...
      The Days Are Evil 37

CHAPTER 5
   Let's Not Be Naïve 51

CHAPTER 6
   A Good Confession Depends Upon
      The Ten Commandments 67

CHAPTER 7
   The Importance Of Frequent Confession
      And Forming Our Consciences 93

CHAPTER 8
   "Lord, That I May See!" 103

CHAPTER 9
   May God Give You Pardon And Peace 117

CHAPTER 10
   The Power Of Grace Within Our Souls 125

APPENDIX 143

BIBLIOGRAPHY 161

INDEX 165

ACKNOWLEDGMENTS

A book is rarely the sole work of a single person.

Special gratitude goes to Rev. Michael Giesler and the late Rev. Salvador Ferigle of the Prelature of the Holy Cross and Opus Dei. Rev. Giesler, of St. Louis, worked with me long distance via phone, mail, and fax, chapter by chapter. Despite his own busy schedule and frequent travel obligations, Fr. Mike provided me with a working outline, wonderful resources, and suggested questions that I incorporated into the beginning of each chapter. Fr. Sal Ferigle, of Boston, graciously allowed me to use his course notes on moral law, sin, and the ten commandments. His material provided a wealth of information that enriched this book.

I am also indebted to friend and fellow writer, Kay King, who enthusiastically reviewed each chapter for grammar and content.

Writing is an occupation of intense concentration. Interruptions can disrupt the thought process and set the writer back hours, sometimes days. It would not have been possible for me to meet my deadline without the help and encouragement of my husband, Bob. He endured many thrown together meals and carry-outs so that the "creative flow" kept flowing. Friends were also understanding when I promised to return phone calls "in three months." These unique friends not only protected my solitude, but they prayed for the success of this book.

This book was drawn from various sources. Special thanks are extended to Henry Holt & Company, Inc. for allowing me to use a line from a lyric in *The Phantom of the Opera* and The National Council of Catholic Men for the use of Fulton Sheen's material. Other publishers that I wish to thank include Scepter Press for allowing me to quote freely from their material, and Tan Books & Publishers, Inc. (P.O. Box 424, Rockford, IL.,) for granting me permission to quote from *THE SINNER'S GUIDE* by Ven. Louis of Granada.

Dedication

This book is dedicated to:

Our Lady, Queen of Peace, who tries to lead *us* to personal and world peace through the Sacrament of Reconciliation.

Blessed Josemaría Escrivá, founder of the Prelature of the Holy Cross and Opus Dei, who taught me to love and value the Sacrament of Confession.

All the priests who are faithful and untiring ministers of the Sacrament of Conversion.

Introduction

As I tried to begin this book, I was frustrated by constant interruptions. Either the telephone or the doorbell rang almost constantly. While this is not unusual in the Budnik household, what *was* unique was the fact that most of the people calling or dropping by were troubled about something. . .either in themselves or in the world. They were looking not only for hope but also for peace.

As I listened to the concerns of each, it struck me that sin was at the root of their concerns and sufferings. Yes, our world *is* in turmoil because people, many oblivious to the fact, have turned away from God, replacing Him with materialism, sensuality, and self. St. Augustine warned that our hearts are restless until they rest in God. As we replace the hunger for God with a hunger for a bigger house, a more luxurious car, expensive vacations, designer clothes, false ambitions, and promiscuous lifestyles, we actually become not only restless, but more miserable. The momentary thrill or happiness turns to anxiety. These goals can never satisfy our souls, so we long or plot for something else. This obsession to find happiness "in all the wrong places" not only causes turmoil in ourselves, but spills over into the world. Fulton Sheen wrote: "When the goal of civilization consists, not in union with the Heavenly Father, but in the acquisition of material things, there is an increase in the potentialities of envy, greed, and war. Divided men then seek a dictator to bring them together, not in the unity of love, but in the false unity of the three P's—Power, Police, and Politics."[1] Could this be reflected in the New World Order we hear so much about?

---

[1]Fulton J. Sheen, Ph.D., D.D., *Peace of Soul* (New York, Garden City Books, 1951), p.8.

Pope John Paul II explains: ". . .man's rupture with God leads tragically to divisions between brothers.

"In the description of the 'first sin,' the rupture with Yahweh simultaneously breaks the bond of friendship that had united the human family. Thus the subsequent pages of Genesis show us the man and the woman as it were pointing an accusing finger at each other. Later we have the brother hating his brother and finally taking his life.

"According to the Babel story, the result of sin is the shattering of the human family, already begun with the first sin and now reaching its most extreme form on the social level.

"No one wishing to investigate the mystery of sin can ignore this link between cause and effect. As a rupture with God, sin is an act of disobedience by a creature who rejects, at least implicitly, the very one from whom he came and who sustains him in life. It is therefore a suicidal act. Since by sinning man refuses to submit to God, his internal balance is also destroyed and it is precisely within himself that contradictions and conflicts arise. Wounded in this way, man almost inevitably causes damage to the fabric of his relationship with others and with the created world. This is an objective law and an objective reality, verified in so many ways in the human psyche and in the spiritual life as well as in society, where it is easy to see the signs and effects of internal disorder.

"The mystery of sin is composed of this twofold wound which the sinner opens in himself and in his relationship with his neighbor. Therefore one can speak of personal and social sin: from one point of view, every sin is personal; from another point of view, every sin is social insofar as and because it also has social repercussions. . . .[E]ach individual's sin in some way affects others."

". . . .[I]t has been possible to say that 'every soul that rises above itself, raises up the world.' To this law of ascent there unfortunately corresponds the law of descent. Consequently one can speak of a communion of sin, whereby a soul that lowers itself through sin drags down with itself the Church and, in some way, the whole world. In other words, there is no sin, not even the most intimate and secret one, the most strictly individual one, that exclusively concerns the person committing it.

With greater or lesser violence, with greater or lesser harm, every sin has repercussions on the entire ecclesial body and the whole human family. . ."[2]

Until we fill our hearts with God and live according to His will for us, we can neither experience peace, nor happiness. Our unhappiness, discontentment, and turmoil will only increase.

Archbishop Sheen notes, "A man who is not at peace with himself will not be at peace with his brother. World wars are nothing but macrocosmic signs of the psychic wars waging inside microcosmic muddled souls. If there had not already been battles in millions of hearts, there would be none on the battlefields of the world. . .

"Given a soul alienated from self, lawlessness follows. . . . Once a man ceases to be of service to his neighbor, he begins to be a burden to him. . . .

"Unhappy souls almost always blame everyone but themselves for their miseries. Shut up within themselves, they are necessarily shut off from all others except to criticize them. . . . This resulting estrangement from one's fellow man is intensified when one begins to live solely for this world. . . Once the material becomes the goal of life, a society of conflicts is born."[3]

As I listened to the various people talk about their concerns, it struck me how Archbishop Sheen described the anxieties of today so accurately 45 years ago!

Is Our Age A Repeat Of The 1500's?

Our world situation also brings St. Thomas More and St. John Fisher to mind. They lived in a time very similar to ours. In 1527 the English political climate was fraught with danger. The Church was not only under attack but was subverted from within by Henry VIII—all because of his sin of lust. This was a shocking turn of events. Prior to this, in 1521, Pope Leo X named Henry "Defender of the Faith" for his treatise denouncing the Lutheran Reformation. Within a short six years, Henry, a married man, fell in love with a young woman. How easy it is to fall from virtue into mortal sin!

[2]John Paul II, *Reconciliation and Penance* (Boston: St. Paul Books & Media, 1984), pp. 34-37.
[3]*Peace of Soul*, op. cit., pp.7-8.

King Henry was determined to divorce his wife, Catherine of Aragon, and marry his pregnant mistress, Anne Boleyn. The Pope told Henry he could not have his valid marriage to Catherine annulled. Determined to have his way, Henry appointed Thomas Cranmer the archbishop of Canterbury and Thomas Cromwell, his spokesman in the House of Commons. Through their devious plotting, Catherine was divorced and Henry married Anne. With all the political intrigue over the divorce and remarriage, the majority of English Catholics did not realize that the English Catholic Church had become Protestant. St. John Fisher, a Bishop later named a Cardinal, was the *only* member of the English hiercharchy to remain faithful to the holy Catholic Church. For his faithfulness, he was beheaded. The majority of the English people passively accepted the Protestant control of their Church. Those who remained Catholic either went into hiding or were martyred.

St. Thomas More, a lawyer, writer, judge, educator, and diplomat rose to become the Lord Chancellor of England, the highest office in his country. Unlike many of the Catholic politicians of today, he did not leave his faith at home when he went to work. Instead, he stood up for God against Henry the VIII. For his loyalty, he lost his high position, his wealth, and finally his life. While awaiting execution in the Tower of London, More wrote a book entitled *The Sadness of Christ*. In this book, he explains that the only person that we can change is ourselves. Intimately involved in almost all aspects of the English realm, More realized how influential personal sanctity is, not only for this life, but also for the next. He writes: "And yet Christ commands us to contemn[4] the loss of the body itself for His sake. 'Do not be afraid,' He says, 'of those who destroy the body and after that can do nothing further. But I will show you the one you should fear, the one to fear: fear Him who, when He has destroyed the body, has the power to send the soul also to Hell. This I tell you, is the one you must fear.'"[5] More's final words were, "I die the King's good servant—but God's first."

Personal sin affects *not only* the sinner but the whole world, as we see in the example of Henry the VIII. Sin *has* a

---

[4]To view or treat with contempt.
[5]Thomas More, *The Sadness of Christ* (Princeton, NJ: Scepter, 1994), pp.47-48.

domino effect. Personal sin destroys marriages, preborn babies, families, friendships, reputations, businesses, political unity, and many times escalates into war. Promiscuity not only destroys the soul, but ravages the body with numerous contagious diseases, some of which are fatal.

What about venial sins? Do they negatively influence our world? *Any* offense against God negatively impacts our lives and the world we live in. No matter how small a sin looks in our eyes, it's a black blot on our souls. Consider this analogy. As I sat down at the computer to begin this book, I spilled some tea on my skirt. It was really just a small spot but it was right in the middle of the skirt. As small as the spot was, my outfit looked dirty. That is how our soul looks to God when we do *our* will, rather than God's will. Each sin, which is a turning away from God, soils our souls. It may seem a small sin to us but it disfigures our souls, affects those around us and those who deal with us.

In the Old Testament, the cumulative effect of personal sin reached such a crescendo that at times God was forced to punish the people. The most well known punishments include Adam and Eve, the Flood, the Tower of Babel, the destruction of Sodom and Gomorrha by fire and brimstone, and the various punishments associated with the Israelites' forty years of wandering in the desert, and the destruction of Jerusalem.

While sin *is* the cause of personal, national, and international turmoil today, God in His goodness has given us a *gift* to restore peace, joy, and happiness to our souls, our relationships and to the world in general. It is the Sacrament of Reconciliation. Few people realize that this great sacrament could also be called the "sacrament of hope." There is no sin that we could possibly commit that God refuses to forgive in the Sacrament of Reconciliation—if we are sorry. We may have difficulty forgiving ourselves but God not only welcomes us back but He hugs us to His heart in this sacrament.

Preparing for confession gives us a chance to examine our lives, our goals, and most importantly, our relationship with God. It's a time to convert, to get our lives on track again by returning to our Loving Father. It's a chance to begin again with a clean slate. No matter how many times we fall, confession, God's gift of compassion, gives us a chance to begin over and over again. Our nature, wounded by Original Sin, is prone to fall. Each of us is going to fall many times each day and throughout our whole lifetime. God, with such understanding tenderness only asks that we struggle against sin and when we fall into it to return swiftly to Him through Sacramental Confession.

In the Sacrament of Reconciliation, God, through the priest, not only forgives our sins, but if the Sacrament is used correctly, it can help us to grow in virtue (good habits) and the love of God. Christ tells us that we must be perfect as the Heavenly Father is perfect. We cannot become perfect without this sacrament.

The Sacrament of Reconciliation, if used frequently, keeps us moving ahead on the path to sanctity. Not only do we grow in holiness, but we experience a deep sense of peace and happiness despite the turmoil around us. As we struggle to live the will of God each day, we will positively influence those around us and act as a leaven in the world by living exemplary lives.

Why Aren't Catholics Making A Difference In The World?

In the US and its territories, there are almost 60 million Catholics. In the world, there are well over one billion. If all these Catholics were *truly* living their faith, receiving the Sacrament of Reconciliation frequently, and striving for holiness what a positive impact we would have on the world and world events! Just look at the power of the humble and holy people living in the world today. What other explanation is there for the tremendous influence of Mother Teresa of Calcutta, John Paul II, Cardinal Sin of the Philippines, Fr. Paul Marx O.S.B., Fr. John Hardon, S.J., or Mother Angelica?

To positively influence the world, we must begin with our relationship with God, then reach out to our families and friends. Not until there is a resurgence of long lines at the Confessional will there be "peace on earth, good will toward men." In contrast, look at the messy lives of some "Catholic" politicians and their negative effect on national policies and world issues. As John Paul II writes, we either influence the world for the good or for the bad. There is no middle road.

Many times I hear people say, "I'm too old to change," or "I am what I am." Blessed Josemaría Escrivá in his book *The Way* chides us, "Don't say, 'That's the way I am—it's my character.' It's your lack of character. Esto vir! Be a man!"[6]

If we use the Sacrament of Reconciliation frequently and with preparation, we *will* change for the better. Our vices will recede, virtue will begin to grow, then flourish, and we will know the peace and joy of living a godly life.

As a cradle Catholic, I have always taken weekly confession for granted. Through this Sacrament of love and mercy I have *absolute* assurance that my sins are forgiven. God, working through the words of the priest, tells me that my sins are forgiven. I never have to worry or wonder if God has forgiven me.

A phone call made me realize how lucky I am to have this reassurance. The conversation began with the usual complaints about the state of the world. While the litany of world problems spilled out, I interrupted my Protestant friend and explained that the situation will only grow worse unless people convert and turn back to God. This led to a discussion of sin. Finally Kath asked in an exasperated tone, "But how do I know if my sins are forgiven?" Her question stunned me. How could she know for sure? I could only reply, "I know for a fact that I am forgiven in confession. As a Protestant, your only recourse is to say a perfect act of sorrow when you commit serious sins."

Fulton Sheen points out, "Peace of soul cannot come from (man) himself, any more than he can lift himself by his own ears. . . .Nothing short of a Divine invasion which restores man to ethical reality can make man happy when he is alone and in the dark."[7]

Confession is that "Divine invasion" that is not only good for our souls and the world, but it is a necessary part of our lives. Blessed Josemaría writes: "Human life is in some way a constant returning to our Father's house. We return through contrition, through the conversion of heart which means a desire to change, a firm decision to improve our life and which, therefore, is expressed in sacrifice and self-giving. We return to our Father's house by means of that sacrament of pardon in which, by confessing our sins, we put on Jesus Christ again and become his brothers, members of God's family.

---

[6]Blessed Josemaría Escrivá de Balaguer, *The Way* (New Rochelle, NY: Scepter, 1985), n.4.
[7]*Peace of Soul*, op. cit., p.10.

"God is waiting for us, like the father in the parable, with open arms, even though we don't deserve it. It doesn't matter how great our debt is. Just like the prodigal son, all we have to do is open our heart, to be homesick for our Father's house, to wonder at and rejoice in the gift which God makes us of being able to call ourselves His children, of really being His children, even though our response to Him has been so poor."[8]

Archbishop Sheen adds, "Unless souls are saved, nothing is saved; there can be no world peace unless there is soul peace. . . . for nothing happens in the external world that has not first happened within a soul."[9]

May this book help you to develop an understanding of this great Sacrament of Reconciliation and its importance in today's world. May it also encourage you to use the sacrament frequently to restore peace and joy in your life. As an added bonus, you will be a pocket of goodness in a troubled world.

After finishing this introduction, I suddenly realized I had written it on October 13, 1996. How fitting, since October 13th is the anniversary date of the famous miracle that occurred during the apparitions of Mary at Fatima, Portugal in 1917. The main message given there was conversion and the repentance of sin.

Mary Ann Budnik
October 13, 1996

---

[8]Blessed Josemaría Escrivá, *Christ is Passing By* (Ireland: Four Courts, 1982), n.65.
[9]*Peace of Soul*, op. cit., p.1.

CHAPTER 1

The Necessity Of Confession

*"I don't do anything really bad.
Why should I go to confession?"*

To understand the importance of the Sacrament of Reconciliation, we have to begin with our purpose in life. Some people believe they are created for fame or fortune. Others believe they have a special destiny still to be discovered. Still others, struggling with mortgage payments and screaming babies, wonder "What's the point of life?"

As Christians, we should realize that life is the boot camp for eternity. Another way of looking at life is that it is similar to the board game Monopoly. One is given certain talents, personality traits, physical characteristics, and disabilities. Then we are placed in a specific country, vocation, and profession or trade. We each have an ever-changing variety of physical, mental, and spiritual contradictions and sufferings to endure. With this mix, we are to strive to grow in virtue so as to win the game of life—eternity with God. No one can voluntarily quit the game without a stiff penalty. The length of time we participate in the game of life is unknown. Death can end the game at any moment. Most importantly, the stakes are high. While our goal should be eternity with God, those who reject this goal do not merely "go to jail," they go to Hell forever. (Yes, Virginia, Hell exists.)

While this description may sound cold and distasteful, life is actually an exciting adventure if lived in union with God. This is one of the best kept secrets in the world. Sadly, few people have the courage or ambition to experience the peace and joy offered by God. The culture that we live in idolizes the body to the exclusion of the soul. Yet it is our soul that animates our body. When God calls our soul home, the body dies. Stop for a minute and consider the billions of dollars spent each year on our bodies to feed, clothe, pamper, and beautify them. Then consider the amount of time used for all these activities. Compare that time and the amount of money spent on the body to the time and money spent on our soul. Let's face it. ***Little time, effort or money is expended on our souls***. This disparity should cause us concern since our souls live for eternity while our bodies will undergo corruption in the near future. We seem to be foolishly investing in the material to the exclusion of the spiritual. Christ warns us, *"For what does it profit a man, if he gain the whole world, but suffer the loss of his own soul?..*[1] *Do not lay up for yourselves treasures on earth, where rust and moth consume, and where thieves break in and steal; but lay up for yourselves treasures in heaven, where neither rust nor moth consumes, nor thieves break in and steal. For where you treasure is, there also will be your heart."*[2]

Christ refers to the kingdom of heaven as the treasure hidden in the field and the pearl of great price.[3] Unfortunately, many people are more interested in the glitter of fool's gold and the state of the stock market than the kingdom of heaven. Their attitude is, "If it's buried treasure, keep it buried!" This is not a new trend. It has been with us since the beginning of time. Jesus stunned his followers when He confided to them, *"Amen I say to you, with difficulty will a rich man enter the kingdom of heaven. And further I say to you, it is easier for a camel to pass through the eye of a needle, than for a rich man to enter the kingdom of heaven."*[4] Once we become wrapped up in the ma-

---

[1]Matt. 16:26.
[2]Matt. 6:19-21.
[3]Matt. 13:44-46.
[4]Matt. 19:23-25.

terial world around us, the spiritual first takes a back seat and then is forgotten in the mad rush to acquire.

Why Are We Here? Why Is Life Filled With Anxieties?

We were born *solely* to know, love, and serve God here on earth, and to be happy with Him in eternity. Fr. Philip Hughes expresses this same thought in another way: "Man is made to be happy eternally, and his eternal happiness is a continuation of the life which he was created to live on earth, a life of loving service of God."[5] This is our purpose for existing. This is our primary goal in life. If we are looking for peace and happiness, then all of our actions, our ambitions, our time, should be centered on this goal. Unfortunately, the majority pursue finite material ambitions. Fulton Sheen explains, "Anxiety and frustration invariably follow when the desires of the heart are centered on anything less than God, for all pleasures of earth, pursued as final ends, turn out to be the exact opposite of what was expected. The expectation is joyous, the realization is disgust. Out of this disappointment are born those lesser anxieties which modern psychology knows so well: but the root of them all is the meaninglessness of life due to the abandonment of...God.

"The alternative to such anxieties consists in letting oneself go, not by a surrender of the spirit to the world, the flesh, and the Devil, but by an act of proper abandonment...to God. Here the basic anxiety of life is transcended in three ways, each of which brings a peace of soul that only the Godloving enjoy: (1) by controlling desires; (2) by transferring anxiety from body to soul; (3) by surrender to the Will of God."[6]

Archbishop Sheen then explains each point. We experience peace when we control the desires that keep knocking at our heart and causing anxieties, frustrations, sadness, and distress. Each of us experiences this frequently, if not daily. Women may long for luxury vacations, jewelry, clothes, household or garden items. Men may crave a promotion, electronic equipment, a red sports car, club membership, boats, guns, or fishing rods. "A religious man [or woman]...overcomes anxiety...by disciplining

[5]Philip Hughes, *The Faith in Practice* (Catholic Doctrine and Life) (London: Longmans, Green and Company, 1948), p.3.
[6]*Peace of Soul*, op. cit., p.19.

the body until it is subject to the spirit, and by submitting the whole personality to God....[7] Once the soul recognizes that it is made for God, it abandons the...idea that every person is to be judged by what he has. There follows, not only a renunciation of evil, but even a voluntary surrender of some things that are lawful, in order that the spirit be freer to love God."[8]

To say "no" to our wants is difficult, but it becomes impossible if we consistently give in to ourselves. To develop the ability to say "no" we should start with small things until our will is strengthened. Then we can take on the larger temptations. To start, we might avoid going to shopping malls and throw away mail order catalogs without looking at them. Subscription magazines and specialized cable TV stations such as *House & Garden* and the Home Shopper can also increase our desires to acquire unnecessary items. We also have to stop comparing ourselves to others. If we do not, we will be trying to "keep up with the Jones." This not only leads to debt, but also to envy and jealousy. Sometimes the desire to acquire an object can become an obsession. One young married woman wanted a gold leaf chandelier with pastel porcelain roses so badly that she convinced her husband that the family could eat hot dogs for a month. This way she could use her grocery money to purchase the silly item. To this day she and her family cannot eat hot dogs!

Sheen's second point is to transfer our concern from the body to the soul, if we want to acquire peace. "Most souls are anxious about the very things they should not be anxious about. Our Divine Lord mentioned at least nine things about which we should not worry: about having our body killed, about what we shall say in the days of persecution when we are called on the carpet before commissars; about whether we should build another barn (or another skyscraper); about family disputes because we accept the faith; about mother-in-law troubles; about our meals, our drinks, our fashions, our stature (Luke 12). He did tell us that we should be very anxious about one thing and one thing only—our souls.[9]

---

[7] 1 Cor. 3:22,23.
[8] *Peace of Soul*, op. cit., p.20.
[9] Matt. 16:26.

"Our Lord does not mean that worldly activities are unnecessary. He only said that if we are anxious about our souls the lesser anxieties would dissolve: *'Seek ye first (not only) the kingdom of God and His justice, and all these things shall be added unto you.'* [10]

The third way to overcome anxieties and develop interior peace is to develop trust in God by freely surrendering our wills to Him. "Many souls....trust only in their own resourcefulness, their own bank account, their own devices. This is particularly true of many families, who consider the rearing of children solely an economic problem, never once invoking the Heavenly Father's Love: they are like a son who in time of need never called on his wealthy father for assistance. The result is they lose many of the blessings reserved for those who throw themselves into the loving arms of God. This law applies to nations as well as individuals....Many favors and blessings are hanging from heaven to relieve our temporal anxieties if we would only cut them down with the sword of our trust in God. Relief from all wrong anxiety comes, not from giving ourselves to God by halves, but by an all-encompassing love...having no will but His." [11]

While mental illness is a reality and a cross that some of us are asked to carry, others may develop depression and psychological problems when they refuse to acknowledge God as the final goal and the purpose of life. Even those of us who know better are torn between doing the will of God and doing our own will. It's not only a daily struggle, it is a minute-to-minute struggle. A friend asked me about this book on confession. I explained my theme of peace and he noted, "It has been my experience as a physician, that some patients with mental disorders would be helped if they went to confession and had good spiritual direction from a priest."

On a personal level I have also seen this. About ten years ago I was introduced to a woman in her mid 30's. She was divorced with two children. Although she held a master's degree, she was living on welfare because of a mental disability. She came in and out of the Church according to her whims. A mu-

---

[10]Luke 12:31; *Peace of Soul*, op. cit., p.23.
[11]Ibid., p.23.

tual friend introduced us and asked if I would help Shannon to get her spiritual life together. For months we met weekly struggling to get her will under control. As she struggled to grow spiritually, she became more consistent in her prayer life. She went back to frequent confession, attended Mass on Sundays and even at times during the week. Her personality began to flower. Shannon became more cheerful, and people began enjoying her company. Within a year, she landed a good state job, was off welfare, and was able to handle her children. It was a powerful lesson for me to see how profoundly the spiritual effects our day-to-day capabilities. When I think of Shannon, the words of Edith Stein come to mind: "Is it really demanding too much to make room in our life for our Savior, so that He may transform our life into His own?"

The word "freedom" is used to cut our moorings from God. Yet true freedom comes from union *with* God. Cardinal Hickey gave a retreat to the Holy Father one Lent. His theme was "Mary at the foot Of The Cross." Hickey explains: "Mary teaches us that in order to find our freedom, we must first 'lose' it by obedience to God's Will. In the logic of the Gospel, harmony with God's Will is the true definition of freedom, indeed, the only definition worthy of the name. Everything contrary to God's Will is destructive of our human dignity and ultimately of our freedom. Harmony with God's Will always means in the first instance victory over sin...She (Mary) knows that in this life we must take our stand near the Cross, for whenever we stray from it, the power of sin again takes hold of our lives, and our freedom, purchased at the price of the Blood of God's Son, is lost. Daily we must take up the Cross and renounce ourselves. Daily we must strive under God's grace to acquire that self-mastery that is the antithesis to the slavery of sin."[12]

In the midst of the material world, Christ calls us back to reality: *"Enter by the narrow gate. For wide is the gate and broad is the way that leads to destruction, and many there are who enter that way. How narrow the gate and close the way that leads to life! And few there are who find it."* [13] Why is this?

---

[12]Cardinal James Hickey, *Mary at the Foot of the Cross* (San Francisco: Ignatius Press, 1989), p.93.
[13]Matt. 7:13-14.

Sin, The Source Of Our Turmoil

St. Paul explains our frustration: *"For we know that the Law is spiritual but I am carnal, sold into the power of sin. For I do not understand what I do, for it is not what I wish that I do, but what I hate, that I do....Now if I do what I do not wish, it is no longer I who do it, but the sin that dwells in me. Therefore, when I wish to do good I discover this law, namely, that evil is at hand for me....*

"Unhappy man that I am! Who will deliver me from the body of this death? The grace of God through Jesus Christ our Lord. Therefore I myself with my mind serve the law of God, but with my flesh the law of sin." [14]

This sad state of affairs came about, as we all know, because of original sin. Man was created to share everlasting happiness with God by sharing in His divine life. We are made to be God's intimate friends because He loves us so intensely. "Hence man was made with powers of knowing and of loving, with powers through which he might know and love God, powers through which he might receive the love lavished on him by his Creator, and through which the divine life might pass into and enrich his own. It was through knowledge of God's love, through the enriching effects upon himself of that love and through his own life of reciprocal love that man was to realize perfect happiness."[15]

That was the plan. Unfortunately, God's gift of freedom was difficult for Adam. Urged on by Satan and his own wife, Eve, Adam rebelled against God. So began our personal, national, and international turmoil because we inherited Adam's original sin.

Fr. Hughes explains: "Adam had sinned. But Adam was not simply any individual man, a being endowed with human nature. Adam was....in a sense, human nature. The sin did not merely affect him as an individual person. It affected also the nature summed up in him. Whatever weakness and loss followed from that sin were realized in human nature as well as in Adam's person. What Adam had to transmit to his descendants,

---

[14] Romans 7:14-25.
[15] *The Faith in Practice*, op. cit., p.13.

i.e., human nature, would necessarily be transmitted as it now was, in the state in which his sin had left it. His descendants would not receive human nature as he had received it, but weakened, a nature weakened from the very moment of transmission by the parent, of reception by the child...

"Adam's sin...did deprive him firstly of that primitive harmony in which he was created, that mastery of mind over body, and of the higher part of the mind over the lower part of the mind, for it destroyed the subjection of man to God...With it there disappeared that exemption from suffering and death... and there disappeared also the supernatural destiny offered to man, namely that he should one day come to the enjoyment of the sight of God Himself....Adam's sin had not destroyed his human nature but it had deprived it of grace and of the effects of grace.

"...Adam's soul had been endowed with the godlike gift of sanctifying grace. Because of this grace, which had made man something holy, his will had been set, as by a habit, towards the execution of the will of God. Now the contrary was true. Man was to be born with his will no longer so inclined to God. Moreover....all the powers of the soul lost their proper subordination to each other. The reason lost what had directed it to Truth, i.e., Prudence no longer governed it. Ignorance began to affect it and to darken its light. The will had no longer a disposition to goodness, i.e., it was not any more informed by Justice, and it became the instrument of malice. The emotions that should assist man to confront what difficulties meet him in his pursuit of good were greatly weakened.... The will, now averted from God, all the powers of the soul likewise in disarray and conflict, turning by a first inclination to the goods of this life beyond what is reasonable, and preferring them to the eternal good—such is the handicap that henceforward must afflict every human being from its very origin and because of its very origin."[16]

The Effects Of Original Sin

When Adam lost sanctifying grace, which is God's life in the soul, original sin took its place. While we can protest that it

---

[16]Ibid, pp.18-20.

is not fair for us to have to suffer because of Adam's sin, we
have no right to supernatural life. It is a *gift*. As a gift, we can
lose it through our own fault.

The effects of original sin and personal sin are all around
us. Pope John Paul II writes: "Among the many other painful
social phenomena of our times one can note:

— The trampling upon the basic rights of the human person, the first of these being the right to life and to a
worthy quality of life, which is all the more scandalous
in that it coexists with a rhetoric never before known on
these same rights.

— Hidden attacks and pressures against the freedom of individuals and groups, not excluding the freedom which
is most offended against and threatened: the freedom to
have, profess and practice one's own faith.

— The various forms of discrimination: racial, cultural, religious, etc.

— Violence and terrorism.

— The use of torture and unjust and unlawful methods of
repression.

— The stockpiling of conventional or atomic weapons, the
arms race with the spending on military purposes of
sums which could be used to alleviate the undeserved
misery of peoples that are socially and economically
depressed.

— An unfair distribution of the world's resources and of
the assets of civilization, ...

"....[T]he church today is experiencing within herself spo-
radic divisions among her own members, divisions caused by
differing views or options in the doctrinal and pastoral field.

"However disturbing these divisions may seem at first sight, it
is only by a careful examination that one can detect their root: It is
to be found in a wound in man's inmost self. In the light of faith
we call it sin: beginning with original sin, which all of us bear
from birth as an inheritance from our first parents, to the sin which
each one of us commits when we abuse our own freedom."[17]

---

[17]*Reconciliation and Penance*, op. cit., pp. 8-9.

Each of us is a sinner. In fact, in the Bible we are told that the just man falls seven times a day. How many times do the rest of us fall each day! Yet, the world we live in has lost the sense of sin. Very little today is considered "sinful." A woman from St. Louis called and was looking for a priest who could give her spiritual direction in confession. I gave her several names of priests and suggested that she take her teen daughters along with her to confession. She replied, "My 17-year-old doesn't believe anything is a sin. It would be almost impossible for me to get her to confession. I might be able to get my younger daughter to go."

Let's consider for a moment *The Index of Leading Cultural Indicators* of William J. Bennett. Bennett found that while 96% of Americans believe in God and 85% identify themselves as Catholics or Protestants, only 28% of Catholics and 20% of Protestants attend Sunday services. He also found that violent crimes since 1960 increased 650%, teen suicides increased 200%, illegitimate births more than doubled, and divorce increased almost 200%. Abortions are listed at 30 million and the marriage rate is down due to couples "living together."

Immorality is so rampant and destructive to society, that the *Wall Street Journal* recently printed an editorial on the problem. It concluded, "Discouraging illegitimate births should certainly top the list of objectives as Congress debates welfare reform this summer. But much more than that is needed. Averting the consequences of rampant illegitimacy will require a conscious change in attitude and behavior on the part of millions of individual citizens. That is why a national conversation about cultural values is needed...."[18]

Pope John Paul II has pointed out the correlation between our loss of the "sense of sin," the decline in the use of the Sacrament of Reconciliation, and the state of the world.

We began this chapter with a simple question that many priests hear. "I don't do anything really bad. Why should I go to confession?" St. John replies, *"If we say we have no sin, we deceive ourselves, and the truth is not in us. If we confess our sins, He is faithful and just and will forgive our sins."* [19]

---

[18]"White Fright," *Wall Street Journal* (New York) June, 19, 1995.
[19]1 Jn. 1:8-9.

One of the things that has always puzzled me was the fact that apparently great sinners protest they are sinless while great saints insist that they are great sinners. This phenomenon will be explained when we discuss the conscience in a later chapter. For the present, let's use the example of a mirror. The farther we are away from a mirror, the better we look. The closer we get, the more imperfections we see. Spiritually, God is our standard. As we grow in holiness, we see more of our defects as we view God's perfections. The farther we are from God, the less we see our defects. We can also compare spiritual blindness to eyesight. Why is it that we look much older when we put on a new prescription of eyeglasses? Suddenly the wrinkles are more visible and the signs of aging are more noticeable. The new prescription gives us better vision but also a rude awaking!

If we use the Sacrament of Reconciliation frequently and correctly, our spiritual blindness will be cured. We will begin to see our imperfections, sins, and defects. We will also learn to struggle to become more Christlike. When I first began to go to spiritual direction in weekly confession, it was a struggle. Mired in the dirty world around me, it was difficult to see what to confess. After all, it seemed that my life was pretty tame in comparison to the rest of the world. When I voiced this in confession, I was duly humbled when the priest began asking me a list of questions. "Do you do this? How about that? And by the way..." By the time the priest completed his list, I was stunned to see that I was guilty of *every* single sin the priest mentioned. None of the sins he listed were mortal sins, but venial sins are still sins, which are a turning away from God.

This confession was actually my wake-up call that I needed to get *my* spiritual life in order. So began the start of my own tedious, ongoing conversion that will end only with death. But what a bonus I got! As I struggled daily I found that peace is the fruit of this struggle. As my life becomes more focused on God I have more interior peace. That does not mean that life isn't chaotic but rather that God gives peace in the midst of chaos to those who struggle to convert. The unknown author of the story below illustrates this point:

"Jesus and I were riding a tandem bicycle. At first, I sat in front; Jesus in the rear. I couldn't see Him, but I knew He was there. I could feel His help when the road got steep. Then one day, Jesus and I changed seats. Suddenly everything went topsy-turvy. When I was in control, the ride was predictable—even boring. But when Jesus took over, it got wild! I could hardly hold on. 'This is madness!' I cried out. But Jesus just smiled—and said, 'Petal!' And so I learned to shut up and pedal—and trust my bike companion. Oh, there are still times when I get scared and I'm ready to quit. But Jesus turns around, touches my hand, smiles, and says, 'Petal!'"

Conversion is not a single, emotionally packed moment or event. Something may trigger our desire to convert but conversion is a daily, ongoing battle we wage to stay focused on God rather than on ourselves and the world.

To acknowledge this is the first step in returning to God. By going to confession, even when we have no mortal sin, we are helped to stay on the right path and to avoid falling into serious sins in the future. It makes us more conscious of how we are living life—are we living it for God or for ourselves?

The Holy Father explains: "In the concrete circumstances of sinful humanity, in which there can be no conversion without the acknowledgment of one's own sin, the Church's ministry of reconciliation intervenes in each individual case with a precise penitential purpose. That is, the Church's ministry intervenes in order to bring the person to the 'knowledge of self'—in the words of St. Catherine of Siena—to the rejection of evil, to the re-establishment of friendship with God, to a new interior ordering, to a fresh ecclesial conversion. Indeed, even beyond the boundaries of the Church and the community of believers, the message and ministry of penance are addressed to all men and women, because all need conversion and reconciliation."[20] And that includes each one of us!

---

[20]*Reconciliation and Penance*, op. cit., p. 32.

CHAPTER 2

How Intensely God Loves You!

"I'm afraid to go to confession. I can't remember how long it's been since my last confession and I'm not sure what to say. Will the priest be upset with me if my last confession was 10 or 15 years ago?

There is absolutely nothing to fear about going to confession. The fact that you are reading this is an indication that God is drawing you back to the sacrament. ". . .Reconciliation is a gift of God, an initiative on His part,"[1] wrote John Paul II, "but we know that God, 'rich in mercy,' like the father in the parable (of the prodigal son), does not close His heart to any of His children. He waits for them, looks for them, goes to meet them at the place where the refusal of communion imprisons them in isolation and division. He calls them to gather about this table in the joy of the feast of forgiveness and reconciliation."[2]

As for not knowing when you made your last good confession, if you can't remember exactly how long it has been, explain this to the priest. He, like Our Lord, will rejoice that you found the courage to return to confession. You are to be congratulated that you are seeking the forgiveness of God. There will be no lectures or censure. As to what to say, that will be covered in subsequent chapters. The formula for making our confession will be explained in Chapter 9. Never let fear be a consideration in your return to the loving embrace of Jesus.

---

[1]*Reconciliation and Penance*, op. cit., p.19.
[2]Ibid, pp.25-26.

13

Our God is a God of endless mercy and love. He loves us so much that He creates breathtaking springs, fresh summers, glorious autumns, and magical winters. . .just for us. Each day He paints a unique sunset across our skies. He showers us with beauty and music in a technicolor world. Most importantly, God gives us people to love who in turn love us. This human love is just a taste of the Divine Love of God.

Furthermore, God loves us so intensely that He could not bear to see us spiritually destroyed by original sin. So He sent His most cherished Son to redeem us through His death on the Cross. Through Christ's redemption, it is now possible for us to become children of God through the Sacrament of Baptism. Through this sacrament, God gives each person an opportunity to spend eternity with Him. The Servant of God, Padre Pio explains: "Baptism brings about a real transformation in us. We die to sin and are grafted onto Jesus Christ in such a way as to live by His very life. At our baptism we receive sanctifying grace which gives us life, a completely heavenly life, making us children of God, brothers of Christ and heirs to heaven."

But God does not stop with these incredible gifts. He understands our fallen nature and knows we need more than one opportunity to return to Him. Jesus knows our daily struggles. He understands that we are sinners, sometimes great sinners. So He has given us the additional gift of the Sacrament of Reconciliation so that He can forgive us "seventy times seven" times. His limitless Mercy is manifested each time we go to confession. There is no sin God refuses to forgive, *if* we are sorry. There is no limit to the amount of times we can confess the same sin. Likewise, there is no sin that we can mention that will scandalize God or the priest who hears our confession. There is nothing that we can say that will shock the priest. He has heard it all before. Embarrassment or shame should never be a consideration as we prepare for confession. Our main concern should be how soon can we get to confession, not "what will the priest say?" Furthermore, God does not hold grudges. He never tires of forgiving us, even when we commit the same sin over and over again.

To prove this point, God fills the pages of the New Testament with examples and parables of His limitless love, mercy, and gentleness to reassure us. In the Gospel of Matthew (18:12-14) Jesus stresses, almost in extreme terms, how He seeks out sinners. *"If a man has a hundred sheep, and one of them stray, will he not leave the ninety-nine in the mountains, and go in search of the one that has strayed? And if he happened to find it. . .he rejoices over it more than over the ninety-nine that did not go astray. Even so, it is not the will of your Father in heaven that a single one of these little ones should perish."*

In the book *He And I,* Gabrielle Bossis states that in a locution Our Lord told her how uniquely precious we are to God, even when we sin: "Don't you understand that I prefer someone who has fallen many times but who despises himself at my feet, to the self-righteous person who thinks he is without fault. My little girl, tell Me every day how sorry you are for any way you have pained Me. Take a steady look at your failures and stains, and offer them to Me so that I may wash them away. Tell Me how weak you are and how often you fail. . .And then go on your way again, trusting in Me day by day. . . .Even if you see no progress at all, be more patient than ever. Be ready to persevere to the very end. Didn't I need that kind of courage as I climbed up the hill to Calvary?"[3]

While we may become discouraged and want to give up on ourselves, God never gives up on us. Again in Matthew (26:47-50) we read of the betrayal of Jesus by Judas. Christ's response to Judas' treachery was an affectionate question, *"Friend, for what purpose have you come?"* In those words was a veiled invitation for Judas to repent and reconcile with his God. Later that same evening, Peter, the leader of the apostles, denies he knows Jesus (Matt. 26:69-75). Two of the chosen twelve betray Jesus yet He responds to them with affection rather than recrimination. Jesus calls Judas friend, to Peter He gives the keys to Heaven.

St. Luke (7:36-38) describes the moving story of the penitent woman, known throughout the area as a great sinner. Knowing Jesus is a guest, she enters the Pharisee's home while the Lord is dining. In front of the assembled guests she humiliates herself by bathing His feet with her tears, drying His feet

---

[3]Gabrielle Bossis, *He and I* (Quebec: Editions Paulines, 1969), p.119.

with her hair and finally anointing them with expensive oils. The host, Simon, disgusted by such a display, is corrected by Our Lord. Jesus concludes by saying, *"I say to you, her sins, many as they are, shall be forgiven her, because she has loved much. But he to whom little is forgiven, loves little."* Turning to the woman, Jesus comforts her by saying, *"Your sins are forgiven. . .Your faith has save you; go in peace."* In the next chapter of Luke we are introduced to Mary Magdalene "from whom seven devils had gone out" (8:2-3). Magdalene, the great sinner, found in Jesus a spiritual love greater than carnal lust. Her conversion was not brought about through the rational arguments of family and friends but through the intensely burning love of God. Once she turned to God, she was faithful to the end. Our Lord, abandoned by almost all, finds Magdalene, racked with sobs, clinging to His cross. Even in death, she visits His tomb where she sees the risen Lord. This great sinner is numbered among the great saints! Luke also records the parable of the lost coin (15:8-10) which Christ concludes by saying, *"Even so, I say to you, there will be joy among the angels of God over one sinner who repents."* This parable is followed by the story of the prodigal son (Lk. 15:11-32) who took his inheritance, squandered it in dissipation, and finally returned home thinking he would work as a hired hand for his father. His father, heartbroken, sees him coming in the distance. Our Lord continues, *". . .his father saw him and was moved with compassion, and ran and fell upon his neck and kissed him. And the son said to him, 'Father, I have sinned against heaven and before you. I am no longer worthy to be called your son.' But the father said to his servants, 'Fetch quickly the best robe and put it on him, and give him a ring for his finger and sandals for his feet, and bring out the fattened calf and kill it, and let us eat and make merry; because this my son was dead, and has come to life again; he was lost, and is found.'"*

The Holy Father points out: "Like the father in the parable, God looks for the return of his child, embraces him when he arrives and orders the banquet of the new meeting with which the reconciliation is celebrated.

"The most striking element of the parable is the father's festive and loving welcome of the returning son: It is a sign of the mercy of God, who is always willing to forgive. Let us say at once: Reconciliation is principally a gift of the heavenly Father. . . .

"The parable. . .is above all the story of the inexpressible love of a Father—God—who offers to his son when he comes back to him the gift of full reconciliation. . . . .The prodigal son, in his anxiety for conversion, to return to the arms of his father and to be forgiven, represents those who are aware of the existence in their inmost hearts of a longing for reconciliation at all levels and without reserve, and who realize with an inner certainty that this reconciliation is possible only if it derives from a first and fundamental reconciliation—the one which brings a person back from distant separation to filial friendship with God, whose infinite mercy is clearly known."[4]

Our Father God rejoices when we return to Him in the Sacrament of Confession because it is an act of honesty and courage on our part. Whether it has been 25 years or a week since our last confession, God delights in us with the same affection as a loving mother. In return for our effort, He showers us with gifts. He clothes us in His forgiveness and bestows the jewel of sanctifying graces. Jesus enwraps our souls in peace and joy and our path is made straight. Free from mortal sin, we can feast once again on the Holy Eucharist. Our God is not a stern, unforgiving God. He is a God of tender mercy and delicate affection. Reconciled to God, we can face life with courage and confidence. While we may dread the idea of going to confession, God rewards us with comfort and peace. After a good confession we can "feel" a weight being lifted from our souls. Interiorly we may even want to shout, "God's forgiven me everything!" Once again, life is not only possible to endure but wonderful.

Consider this: even in the midst of the unbearable suffering of the crucifixion, Christ saves the soul of the "good thief." His body racked by indescribable torment, his lifeblood draining onto the ground, Jesus painfully turns his head to face the good thief who implores, "Lord, remember me when you come into your kingdom." Gasping for breath, Jesus tenderly responds, *"'Amen I say to you, this day you shall be with me in paradise'"*

---

[4]*Reconciliation and Penance,*, op. cit., pp.18-19.

(Lk 23:39-43). Just as the dying Jesus was so tender to this sinner, He will likewise be gentle toward us in the confessional. After all, He died specifically to save *us* from our sins.

St. John relates the story of Jesus' compassionate treatment of the Samaritan Woman at Jacob's well (4:1-42). It is to this woman, who had five husbands and was at that time "living with a man," that Jesus reveals He is the Messiah. He gently leads her through their conversation to seek the truth and live an upright life. John also relates the story of the woman caught in adultery (8:1-11). As the people prepare to stone her to death according to the Law of Moses, Jesus is asked His opinion. The adulteress is saved from both spiritual and bodily death when Jesus responds, *"Let him who is without sin among you be the first to case a stone at her."* As people turn to leave, Jesus asks the woman, *"'Has no one condemned you?' She replied, 'No one, Lord.' Then Jesus mercifully replies, 'Neither will I condemn you. Go your way, and from now on sin no more.'"* Jesus, the God-man, gives no recriminations, no lengthy lectures just affectionate, merciful guidance and the woman's heart melts in gratitude.

In the Acts of the Apostles we read how St. Paul persecuted the followers of Christ (9:1-9). He took part in the murder of St. Stephen, yet once he meets Christ on the road to Damascus, he is converted. Today his stature almost equals St. Peter's.

It's Possible For Great Sinners To Became Great Saints!

In the last two thousand years, Church history records many stories of great sinners who through reconciliation with God became great saints. The lives of these saints are not to strike us with awe but to serve as practical examples of how the transforming love of God takes sinners and fashions them into saints. God likewise longs to form us into saints who will spend an eternity of bliss with Him. As Robert Louis Stevenson once wrote, "The saints are the sinners who keep on trying." Let's briefly examine the love stories of some such saints.

St. Monica, as a teenager, was given the job of getting the wine for the family each day. Although she really didn't like the taste, she would take a few sips each time she collected it in the

[5]Augustine, *Confessions* (Book Nine, VIII, p. 196).

cellar. Each day she would sip a little more until her son Augustine relates, "She fell into the habit, so that she would drink off greedily cups almost full of wine."[5] It was only when a slave girl called her a drunkard that she reformed. At the age of 22, she was married to a promiscuous pagan who was 33 years her senior. If this wasn't bad enough, her husband became violent when angry. Her brilliant son, Augustine, was not only a heretic but was sexually active by the age of 15. While still in his teens he took a mistress and fathered a son by the age of 18. This was not a passing affair. Augustine lived with this woman for 15 years. Think of all the emotions, temptations, and discouragement Monica had to fight! She persevered and won the conversion of her husband on his deathbed and the conversion of her son after 17 years of constant prayer. In the ups and downs of daily living, Monica, the reformed drinker, became a saint.

Her son, Augustine, was a difficult case. He was besieged by the sins of intellectual pride and lust. He realized that eventually he would have to give up his mistress "but not yet." Augustine, despite the multitude and diversity of his sins, with reluctance eventually traded his earthly love for a greater Love. He converted, grew in holiness, and became not only a great saint, but the greatest doctor of the Western Church. As Msgr. Leon Cristiani writes, Augustine, "A man of rare genius, [was] destined to be a saint. Not a ready-made saint, but one who fought his way slowly out of his carnal passions to perfect chastity, who sank from error to error before finding the lodestar of divinely revealed Truth. And finally a man who emerged from the infernal isolation of egoism, sin, and irreligion into the incomparable fellowship of God-Trinity."[6]

Mary of Egypt is also a powerful example of how it is possible to shake off the past and return to God. She left home, without her parents permission, at the age of twelve and went to Alexandria where she lost her innocence. For seventeen years she lived submerged in immorality until she felt compelled to return to the waiting arms of her God. Rev. Winfrid Herbst explains, "How sad it is when innocence and virtue are lost through mortal sin! But such should never lose heart; God for-

[6]Msgr. Leon Cristiani, *The Story of Monica and Her Son Augustine* (Boston, St. Paul Editions, 1977), p. 15.

gives and forgets, no matter how deep the fall, if only with a humble and contrite heart we turn to Him for mercy, let our soul be washed anew in His Precious Blood in the Sacrament of Penance, and begin bravely to serve Him with virtue regained."[7]

Blessed Matt Talbot was born in Dublin in 1856. He began drinking at the age of twelve when he left school and took a job as a messenger boy. Rather than being paid in checks or cash, many times Irish laborers were given drafts to be cashed at certain pubs where the foreman would get a cut of the money spent on drinks. Matt would go to cash his $4 a week pay at the pub and stay to drink it up. He claimed his body continuously craved alcohol. Broke one week and desperate for a drink he approached some friends hoping they would buy him a drink. They ignored him. That was the turning point for 28 year old Matt. Away from the Church for years, he first went to confession then took the pledge to abstain from alcohol. Although he did not know how he could keep the pledge for a day, with the grace of God he kept it one day at a time for forty-one years.

In confession our compassionate Jesus cleanses us from our sins and fills our hearts with peace and joy. With Jesus, we have nothing to fear. He is Patience, Gentleness, Compassion, Mercy and Love. To prevent intimidation and fear, Christ does not demand that we face the awesome majesty of God to be forgiven. Instead, He uses the priest, a sinner like ourselves. John Paul II writes in *Reconciliation and Penance*: "It is the act of the prodigal son who returns to his father and is welcomed by him with the kiss of peace. It is an act of honesty and courage. It is an act of entrusting oneself, beyond sin, to the mercy that forgives. . . .The sacramental formula 'I absolve you' and the imposition of the hand and the Sign of the Cross made over the penitent show that at this moment the contrite and converted sinner comes into contact with the power and mercy of God. It is the moment at which, in response to the penitent, the Trinity becomes present in order to blot out sin and restore innocence. And the saving power of the passion, death and resurrection of Jesus is also imparted to the penitent as the 'mercy stronger than sin and offense,' . . .God is always the one who is princi-

---

[7]Rev. Winfrid Herbst, S.D.S., *Follow the Saints* (New York: Benziger Brothers, 1933), p.55.

pally offended by sin. . .and God alone can forgive. Hence the absolution that the priest, the minister of forgiveness, though himself a sinner, grants to the penitent is the effective sign of the intervention of the Father in every absolution and the sign of the 'resurrection' from 'spiritual death' which is renewed each time that the sacrament of penance is administered. Only faith can give us certainty that at that moment every sin is forgiven and blotted out by the mysterious intervention of the Savior."[8]

The Hound Of Heaven

Fulton Sheen tells us: "The two greatest dramas of life are the soul in pursuit of God and God in pursuit of the soul. . .[T]he soul that pursues God can do it leisurely. . .But when God pursues the soul, He proves a Relentless Lover, Who will never leave the soul alone until He has won it or been conclusively denied."[9]

While God's pursuit of our soul may be difficult to see, often we can see His love as He pursues others. I saw it in an elderly woman, grown self-centered and cantankerous, when she was reunited to the Church on her deathbed. I heard it in the voice of a radical feminist theologian. She still holds many heretical views, but suddenly it bothers her that she had joined the dissenters' vocal defiance of *Humanae Vitae* in the '60s. "What gave them the authority to defy the Holy Father and split the Church?" she now asks. God is clearly pursuing her. The Divine Lover also pursued a young man when he left the Catholic Church right out of high school. He became an atheist when he fell in with the political radicals while attending college in Berkeley, California. Years later, the study of economics not only changed his political and economic views but was instrumental in bringing him back to the Church. God did not stop there. The young man was ordained a priest and is now a lecturer and writer. His articles are published in the *Wall Street Journal*.

While these antidotes are dramatic, God works just as dramatically in each of our lives. We just might not be aware of it.

Archbishop Sheen points out that the soul tries to escape from God through "the unconscious mind, sex, science, nature,

---

[8]*Reconciliation and Penance*, op.cit., pp.81-82.
[9]Fulton, J. Sheen, Ph.D., DD, *Lift Up Your Heart*, op. cit., p.287.

and humanism. These five substitutes for God are chosen in an effort to preserve the ego. . .from the shattering contact of Divinity."[10]

"The search for peace within the self is always doomed to fail; the two loneliest places in the world are a strange city and one's own ego. When a man is alone with his thoughts, in false independence of the Love Who made him, he keeps bad company."[11] Subconsciously society knows this, and flees from silence via constant radio, TV, and Walkmans. It's rare to call a home or business and not hear some music or talk show blaring in the background. While people give excuses, the fact is God's voice speaks to us in silence. Fearing to hear what He says, we drown Him out with noise.

Archbishop Sheen continues: "The second escape by which souls try to find fulfillment without God is sex. . .An age of religious anarchy is always a licentious age, and a period of political confusion, too: this is because a rebellion against the Divine Law affect both society and man. When a people have lost sight of the meaning and purpose of life, they then attempt to find compensation in the intensity of their experiences, either revolutionary or personal. The 'thrill' is sought for itself. Real love attaches itself to a single, unique personality and remains loyal, nontransferable; but sexual enjoyment, if it is a goal in itself, leads to promiscuity. . . ."[12]

We can try to escape through nature and science, but God is the Author of both. Humanism can hold our heart and attention only briefly because it has no substance. "Even though one is convinced of the emptiness of life and suspects that God might fill that void, there is still a great obstacle to be surmounted on the road to peace; and that obstacle consists of self-discipline, mortification, and penance. . . .Our Lord is always forbidding to those who see Him only from a distance."[13]

Archbishop Sheen concludes by saying, "Many know the anxiety of a bad conscience; few know the peace of a good con-

---

[10]Ibid, p.288.
[11]Ibid, p. 288, p.290.
[12]Ibid, pp. 291-292.
[13]Ibid, p.299.

science. . . If God's displeasure is so terrible that it keeps the guilty awake at night, think of the joys that beckon in His Pleasure! If it is misery to be under His wrath, then it is ecstasy to be under His Love!. . .

"Love of the Lord is greater in realization than in desire. . . .the Cross frightens us; the sacrifice of selflessness and sin seems like a little death; non-sensual love appears as lovelessness. But after one makes the surrender. . .one is possessed of a joy that is ineffable, that beggars all description. The discovery makes one act so differently that his friends think he has lost his mind; but actually, he has found his soul, which the believer would not now give up for anything in all the world."[14]

There was a young woman who entered a church at confession time. Observers could tell she was upset by her jerky, quick movements, the expression and perspiration on her face. She would approach the confessional, then rapidly turn and walk back toward the church doors. Then she would stop, turn and walk again toward the confessional, only to repeat her previous flight toward the church doors. She did this several times until she finally mustered the courage to walk into the confessional. When the young woman emerged, her face was wreathed in smiles. She had found the courage to be forgiven and loved. In return she found peace and joy.

Our loving Jesus reportedly told a mystic, "Write, I don't want people to be afraid of Me any more, but to see My heart full of love and to speak with Me as they would with a dearly beloved brother.

"For some I am unknown. For others, a stranger, a severe master or an accuser. Few people come to Me as to one of a loved family. And yet My love is there, waiting for them. So tell them to come, to enter in, to give themselves up to love just as they are. Just as they are. I'll restore them. And they will know a joy they have never known before. I alone can give that joy. If only they would come! Tell them to come. . ."[15] Won't you come and experience the goodness of our God?

---

[14]Ibid, p.307., p. 305.
[15]*He and I*, op. cit., p. 60.

CHAPTER 3

Reconciliation Is A Priceless Gift From God

"I tell my sins directly to God. God, who is good, will forgive me. Why should I tell my sins to a priest, who is a mere human being? Confession is a man-made rule in the Catholic Church. Nowhere in the Bible does it say that Jesus instituted confession as a sacrament."

When our first parents turned away from God in the Garden of Eden, God could have abandoned us. Instead, He promised to send a Redeemer to save us from our sins. Throughout the Old Testament there is a foreshadowing of the Sacrament of Reconciliation. In fact, did not God anticipate Adam's confession when He asked him, "Have you eaten of the tree?" Adam's son Cain was also invited to confess, when God interrogate him: "Where is your brother?" Later in the Bible we read of burnt offerings in the Mosaic law that were used as sin offerings. The great king, David, confessed his sin of adultery with Bethsabee to Nathan, the prophet, who then gave him a penance. In the New Testament, John the Baptist heard the confessions of those who came to have their sins removed by his baptism of water. And Zacchaeus, the Publican, made a public confession to Our Lord. Jesus not only worked miracles but gave absolution for sins *before* curing the various people in the Gospels.

While the world waited for the Savior, frail human nature continued to say "no" to God. *"The Lord saw that the wickedness of man was great in the earth....'I will destroy man, whom I have created, from the face of the earth....'"* [1] And so God punished humanity with the great flood saving only Noah and his family. Even this did not seem to leave a lasting impression on humanity. After this major punishment (our news media would call it a natural disaster), if we page through the Bible, we see example after example of man's infidelity to God and God's limitless patience and love toward man. *"Let the wicked man forsake his way and return to the Lord, and He will have mercy on him because He is generous in forgiving."* [2] They who are anxious to reconcile to God are promised: *"I will take the heart of stone from their bodies and I will give them a heart of flesh, so that they may walk according to my laws; thus they shall be my people and I will be their God. But as for those whose hearts are devoted to their detestable abominations, I will bring down their conduct upon their heads, says the Lord God."* [3]

The love of God reaches its zenith at the crucifixion. For the love of us, Jesus Christ, true God and true man, sheds *every* single drop of blood in His most holy body to redeem us from our sins. God wanted to show in the most dramatic way possible the magnitude of His love for us. Our love is *so* small compared to God's. Consider how irritated we become when we have to run an unexpected errand for a spouse, relative, or friend. Christ saved us because He loves us without limit. Although He gave His life for us, He knew that our wounded nature would still need ongoing help to reach unity with Him in eternity. That is why Christ instituted the Sacrament of Reconciliation.

"Confession is a man-made rule in the Catholic Church. Nowhere in the Bible does it say that Jesus instituted confession as a sacrament."

The sacrament of confession was not made by men, but by the God-man Jesus Christ. Just as Christ instituted Baptism and the Eucharist, He instituted the Sacrament of Confession. This is clear in the biblical texts of St. John (20:21-23) and St. Matthew (16:18-19) where Christ confers the power to forgive sins upon His disciples. Let's consider these and other texts.

At the Last Supper, Our Lord set the groundwork for this great sacrament of mercy when He told the Apostles that He would send His Spirit to convict the world of sin. [4] "It is only

---

[1] Genesis 6:5-7.
[2] Isaiah 55:7
[3] Ezekiel 11:19-21.
[4] John 16:8.

through the Spirit of Christ that we know we are sinners," Bishop Sheen stated, "and it is His voice which calls us to repentance. We may make our confessions because our conscience urges us to do so, but the voice that speaks to us is the voice of the Holy Spirit telling us of God's mercy and love and righteousness...."[5]

After the Resurrection, Christ appeared to His disciples telling them: *"Receive the Holy Spirit; whose sins you shall forgive, they are forgiven them; and whose sins you shall retain, they are retained."* [6] It is at this moment that Christ gave the Church His authority to forgive sins.

The Holy Father writes: "The Lord Jesus Christ, physician of our souls and bodies, who forgave the sins of the paralytic and restored him to bodily health, has willed that His Church continue, in the power of the Holy Spirit, His work of healing and salvation, even among her own members."[7]

Christ gave us this sacrament to unburden the soul and conscience. It is like a spiritual bath. Sin blackens our souls while filling them with a spiritual stench. Some of the saints could actually "smell" the souls of people in mortal sin. St. Catherine of Siena was one such saint. At times, the smell of mortal sin became so intense around certain people that she became physically ill. Confession scrubs our souls "whiter than white," removes the stench while replacing it with interior peace.

Confession not only purifies the soul, but it infuses sanctifying grace (God's life) along with sacramental grace to help us overcome the tendencies that lead to committing the same sins time after time.

"I tell my sins directly to God. God, who is good, will forgive me."

What assurance do we have that God will forgive us outside of confession? God sent His Son Jesus Christ to redeem us and

---

[5]Fulton J. Sheen, *These are the Sacraments* (New York: Hawthorn Books, Inc. 1962), pp.69-70.
[6]John 20:21-23.
[7]John Paul II, Encyclical Letter *"On the Holy Spirit in the Life of the Church and the World"* (Dominum Et Vivificantem), nn.27-48.

to give us the sacraments of salvation. If we do not use Christ's sacraments, it is presumptuous of us to think we are forgiven.

Our ways of experiencing reconciliation are not God's ways. John Paul II points out: "...[F]or a Christian the sacrament of penance is the ordinary way of obtaining forgiveness and the remission of serious sin committed after baptism. Certainly the Savior and His salvific action are not so bound to a sacramental sign as to be unable in any period or area of the history of salvation to work outside and above the sacraments. But in the school of faith we learn that the same Savior desired and provided that the simple and precious sacraments of faith would ordinarily be the effective means through which His redemptive power passes and operates. It would therefore be foolish, as well as presumptuous, to wish arbitrarily to disregard the means of grace and salvation that the Lord has provided and, in the specific case, to claim to receive forgiveness while doing without the sacrament that was instituted by Christ precisely for forgiveness...."[8]

Some people contend that confession "is pre-Vatican II." Contrary to their belief, Vatican II document *Lumen Gentium* teaches that: "Those who approach the sacrament of Penance obtain pardon from God's mercy for the offense committed against Him, and are, at the same time, reconciled with the Church which they have wounded by their sins and which by charity, by example, and by prayer labors for their conversion."[9]

Those who refuse to go to confession or consider it unnecessary, may not only be presumptuous but also maybe proud or lack courage. It takes humility to admit that we have turned away from God. It takes courage to prepare for confession and then lay our soul bare before Christ in the person of the priest. Unfortunately few Americans seem to have the courage or the humility to go to confession. According to an Associated Press report, "[T]he Committee for Pastoral Research and Practices of the National Conference of Catholic Bishops surveyed 2,500 priests, 2,850 active lay Catholics and about 380 bishops in...1988. The majority of the Catholics surveyed, 55 percent,

---

[8]*Reconciliation and Penance*, op. cit., n.31, III pp.77-79.
[9]LG 11& 2.

said they went to confession once or twice a year. Four percent said they went once a week, 5 percent said they went monthly, and 17 percent said every two or three months. Nineteen percent said they never celebrated the sacrament.

"The bishops attributed the decline in confessions to a less pervasive sense of sin, confusion about what is morally right and wrong and disagreement with the Church's moral teaching...."[10]

The Sacrament of Reconciliation not only cleanses our souls but also provides a spiritual "check-up" and a pep talk for the future. Christ, through the priest, gives the penitent advice on how to avoid similar sins in the future. There is no other place where we can receive such personal spiritual advice and guidance. A non-Catholic once told my son-in-law, "You Catholics have your confession, we have our psychiatrists." Catholics have the better deal. A psychiatrist cannot forgive a burdened conscience, infuse grace to elevate the soul, counsel with the authority of Christ, give a penance to symbolize our debt repayment, and leave us with a feeling of relief and gratitude. While psychiatrists charge outrageous fees, we get all of the above free by virtue of our baptism and membership in the Catholic Church. Such a fabulous, personalized gift, yet so few people take advantage of it!

"Why should I tell my sins to a priest, who is a mere human being?"

The priest is only a man, a sinner like all of us...but in the moment of giving absolution he is Christ Himself, who forgives us. This is possible through the power of ordination since Christ gave this power to the first apostles and their successors throughout time. Still, it is common to hear people say, "I don't have to confess my sins to a man! I go directly to God." The **Catholic Catechism** begs to differ: "Confession to a priest is an essential part of the Sacrament of Penance."[11] Unless a confession is "heard" how can a priest absolve a sinner? How can a penance be given if the offense is not known? As for the state-

---

[10]David Briggs, "Survey On Confession Shows Different Views," *The State Journal Register* (Springfield, IL), March 11, 1990, p. 10.
[11]*Catholic Catechism*, op. cit. #1456.

ment that we tell our sins to a man, a man does not have the power to forgive sins. Only a validly ordained priest with jurisdiction (that is, with power given to him by the bishop) can forgive sins in Jesus' name. In the Sacrament of Reconciliation we do *not* confess our sins to a mere mortal. We whisper our transgressions to Christ Himself through the ears of the priest, His representative. Our Lord is reported to have told Blessed Faustina: *"Daughter... Every time you go to confession, immerse yourself entirely in My mercy, with great trust, so that I may pour the bounty of My grace upon your soul. When you approach the confessional, know this, that I Myself am waiting there for you. I am only hidden by the priest, but I myself act in your soul."* [12]

If we could only remember this, we would not be embarrassed when a priest, who might also be our friend, is hearing confessions. Sometimes people actually put off going to confession until they find a priest who does not know them or their voice. They fear the priest friend will think less of them after confession. This is not true! It is only pride rearing its ugly head.

It is possible that in the past we may have been hurt by a impatient or gruff priest in confession. Some even claim this as their reason for leaving the faith. Maybe the priest did not understand us. He may have been out of sorts that day. Maybe he didn't share our viewpoint of the seriousness of a certain sin. And yes, maybe we didn't want to hear what he had to say regarding something we didn't feel was a serious offense. While the priest represents Christ, his humanness can sometimes intrude. This should never discourage us from returning to the Sacrament of Reconciliation. Choose another priest. Ask friends for the name of a good confessor. Never permit fear of confession to keep you from the fount of God's mercy.

Since the priest acts in Christ's name, he is bound by the seal of confession. Nothing that we say in confession can ever be repeated—even if the priest is threatened with death. Also, many priests maintain that once they leave the confessional, what they heard is wiped from their minds.

---

[12]Blessed M. Faustina Kowalska, *Divine Mercy In My Soul,* (Stockbridge: Marian Press, 1987), #1602

Our Lord conferred the power to forgive sins on Peter when he told him: *"You are Peter, and upon this rock I will build my Church, and the gates of hell shall not prevail against it. And I will give you the keys of the kingdom of heaven; and whatever you shall bind on earth shall be bound in heaven, and whatever you shall loose on earth shall be loosed in heaven."* [13] This promise to Peter was later followed up after the Resurrection with a similar promise to the Apostles, which we considered earlier in this chapter. The person who holds the keys to a city, controls the city. Our Lord is giving Peter authority not only over His Church, but also over the entrance of souls into Heaven.

St. Paul confirms this when he writes: *"But all things are from God, who has reconciled us to Himself through Christ and has given to us the ministry of reconciliation."* [14]

The **Catechism of the Catholic Church** expands on this idea: "Since ancient times the bishop...has...been considered ...the one who principally has the power and the ministry of reconciliation:...Priests, his collaborators, exercise it to the extent that they have received the commission either from their bishop (or religious superior) or the Pope...."[15]

Consider what a difficult sacrament this is for priests. The priest sits in a space that is not well ventilated and poorly lit waiting for penitents to come. The priest, as mediator between God and man, should not only be in the state of sanctifying grace himself, but should prepare to hear confessions through prayer and sacrifice. He patiently listens to offense after offense to a God he not only loves, but to whom he has given his life. When needed, the priest must have the courage to explain the full moral teaching of the Catholic Church. This can be difficult at times. For example, I suggested to a group of friends a wonderful priest for confession. The women wrote down the days and times the priest was available. One Saturday morning I was rudely awakened by a call from one of the women. She was furious with me. She had gone to confession on Thursday. During the course of her confession, she disclosed the fact that she used

---

[13]Matt. 16:18-19.
[14]2 Cor. 5:18.
[15]*Catechism of the Catholic Church*, op. cit., n. 1462.

an IUD for contraception. The priest courageously explained the evil of contraception and then added that IUDs also act as abortifacients. Although she adamantly refused to follow the Church's teachings on contraception, she was angry with me for "burdening her conscience"!

Likewise, we should not tempt the priest to compromise the truth out of human respect or sympathy for the cross Our Lord may be asking us to carry.

As we have seen, this sacrament is a difficult one for priests with the time commitment, the physical uncomfortableness, and the moral obligation to penitents. If it was a man-made sacrament, it would have been discontinued centuries ago!

As discussed in the Introduction, sin is not only personal. It affects all of society. "Every sinner is blameworthy, not only in regard to himself, but also in regard to the Church, and first and foremost to God. If he is ever to recover, it can only be by the intervention of the Church, and by an intervention of God....The priest, acting as the representative of the Church welcomes back the penitent to the community of believers....The priest re-establishes the sinner in grace; he restores the sinner to his rights as a son of the Eternal Father; he reconciles him not only to God, but also to God's society of the Church...." [16]

The priest is not just a mere human being. There are so many edifying stories of heroic priests who put their lives on the line to bring the sacraments and spiritual comfort to their spiritual brothers and sisters. This is one of my favorite. One night a priest, who lived during the French revolution, was secretly summoned by the family of a man who was known for his fierce hatred of the Catholic Church. When the dying man realized who his visitor was, he cursed and raged and said to the priest, "Don't you know who I am? I hate priests. I have strangled a dozen of them with my bare hands."

"No," the priest replied, opening his collar and showing the man the marks on his throat, "you only killed 11. I survived your attack and now I'm here to prepare you for death." The man was so moved by the priest's courage that he repented of his sins and asked for God's mercy and forgiveness.

---

[16]*These are the Sacraments*, op. cit., pp.75-76.

One of our parish priests tells the story of visiting a dying man who was a hardened sinner. He asked the man if he could hear his confession. The man snarled, "Leave me to Hell!" The priest, grabbing a chair, sat down. "Well, I've never seen anyone go to Hell before. Do you mind if I sit and watch?" The dying man was so startled that he made a good confession and received the last rites. How blessed we are to have such priests!

Frequent Confession Prepares Us For Eternity

Life is so fleeting. For those who are young, life seems to stretches ahead almost to eternity. For those who have hit the "over the hill" forty's, we realize that eternity can begin for us in an instant——a sudden car crash, an explosion, an earthquake, a flash flood, or a terminal illness. At the moment of death, our soul stands before the Throne of God to be judged. The best preparation for that certain event in our future is frequent confession. By frequenting the sacrament, we refine our conscience, grow in virtue, fight our vices (bad habits), and are infused with God's grace. By discussing our spiritual struggle with the priest, he can give us sound advice and encouragement on how to battle our vices and grow in virtue. Feel free to talk over anything with the priest.

If we have not committed a mortal sin, is it even necessary to go to frequent confession for venial sins? The *Catholic Catechism* responds: "Without being strictly necessary, confession of everyday faults (venial sins) is nevertheless strongly recommended by the Church...[T]he regular confession of our venial sins helps us form our conscience, fight against evil tendencies, let ourselves be healed by Christ and progress in the life of the Spirit."[17]

As we grow in virtue, and fight our bad habits (vices) our personality develops. We become happier, more pleasant to be around. We take ourselves less seriously, are filled with hope, and even develop a sense of humor. We also become more sensitive to the needs and concerns of others such as our spouse, family, relatives, friends, and business associates. We become less inclined to think of ourselves and our wants. It takes less effort to do works of charity and the spiritual and corporal

---

[17]*Catechism of the Catholic Church*, op. cit. #144458.

works of mercy. In other words, we become less *selfish* and more *selfless*. Our marriage is enriched and happier, family life is a joy rather than unending problems, and people gravitate to us in friendship. Most importantly, we are at peace with God and with those around us. We become leaven in society, a light in the midst of a dark world. Considering this why would anyone *want* to avoid confession?

Last Chance Charlies

Some people would rather not think about the consequences of their lives in relation to eternity. They live for the here and now while confession means an ongoing conversion. Not only does this sound distasteful, it also means hard work. Some figure when the time to die arrives (certainly in the distant future), they will experience a deathbed conversion and come back to God. Or, God in His unlimited mercy will forgive their transgressions without their efforts. This is the sin of presumption.

What do the saints have to say on this subject? St. Gregory warns, "God promises to receive the repentant sinner when he returns to Him, but nowhere does He promise to give him tomorrow." St. Caesarius adds: "Some say, 'In my old age I will have recourse to penance'; but how can you promise yourself an old age, when your frail life cannot count with security upon one day?"

The quote that impresses me the most is from Ecclesiasticus: *"Delay not to be converted to the Lord, and defer it not from day to day. For His wrath shall come on a sudden and in the time of vengeance He will destroy you."* [18]

By delaying our conversion, we are making it more difficult to come back to God. Without confession the old vices grow stronger (and we all have them). The longer we wait to attack our vices, the harder the battle. In contrast, frequent confession eats away at our vices. St. Bernard claims, "When a vice is confirmed by habit it cannot be extirpated except by a very special and even miraculous grace." Venerable Louis of Granada preached, "Therefore, there is nothing which a Christian should dread more than a habit of vice, because...once that is established it is almost impossible to root it out. A second cause of

---

[18]Ecclus. 5:8-9.

this difficulty is the absolute power which the devil has over a soul in sin. Satan is the strongly armed man mentioned in the Gospel, who does not easily relinquish what he has acquired....

"Another cause of this difficulty is the separation which sin makes between God and the soul....God withdraws further and further from a sinful soul, in proportion as her vices increase...

"The last cause of this difficulty is the corruption of sin, which weakens and impairs the faculties of the soul, not in themselves, but in their operations and effects. Sin darkens the understanding, excites the sensual appetites, and, though leaving it free, so weakens the will that it is unable to govern us....How, then, can you think your conversion will be easier in the future, since every day increases the obstacles you now dread, and weakens the forces with which you must combat them?....If you are now baffled by a year or two of sinful habits, how can you resist their strength at the end of ten years?"[19]

How true those words are! One couple we befriended decades ago had a mixed marriage. The wife was strongly attracted to the Catholic Church. Betsy confided that in time she would convert to Catholicism but she had to wait until the "change of life" because she had all the children she wanted (three) and was using contraception. She told me that she could have the best of both world—three children and in time the Catholic faith. Betsy's youngest child is now 28 years old and Betsy has gone through "the change" but she still is a Protestant. The years of violating God's law have taken its toll. Betsy has lost the gift of faith. When we put off today what we know is right for tomorrow, "tomorrow" may never come for us. When we chose to ignore the grace of God or defer it to the future, we may lose the gift for eternity. The longer we wait to rectify sin in our lives, the more evil our souls accumulate. Each time we say "no" to God we are flinging Satan's words back into God's face—"I will not serve!" How can we presume God's mercy when we treat Him with constant ingratitude in our daily lives?

While confession remits eternal punishment for our sins, we still have to deal with the temporal punishment. We can do this

---

[19]Venerable Louis of Granada, *The Sinner's Guide* (Rockford, IL: Tan Books and Publishers, Inc., 1985), pp. 189-191.

either now on earth, or in Purgatory. Since we are told that the greatest pain on earth is not even equal to the smallest pain in Purgatory, the wise person will seek to do reparation on earth now so as to avoid Purgatory in the future.

For those planning a deathbed conversion, St. Isidore cautions: "If you have a hope of being pardoned for your sins at the hour of death, do penance for them while you are able. But if you spend your life in wickedness, and still hope for forgiveness at your death, you are running a most serious risk. Though you are not sure that you will be damned, your salvation is by no means more certain."

A bumper sticker seen in Knoxville, Tennessee makes one think: "Eternity—Your Choice—Smoking or non-smoking."

CHAPTER 4

Look Carefully Then How You Walk. . . The Days are Evil [1]

"With regard to certain sins, one priest says one thing, and another priest disagrees. Why go to confession, if there are so many different theories about sin? Also, specifically, how do we sin?"

Unfortunately, there is confusion in the Church today. St. Peter warns us: *"There will be false teachers among you. These will seek to introduce disastrous heresies and will even set themselves against the Master who ransomed them. Many will listen to them and will follow their licentious ways. Through their offense, the Christian faith will be reviled. In their greed, they will exploit you with fabrications."* [2] In spite of today's spiritual turmoil, we know from natural law that there is only one truth and that truth never changes. With our intellect and free will, we have the ability to learn the truth and the grace to follow it despite the negative influences surrounding us.

St. Paul also wrote on this same topic so that we will be prepared rather than scandalized. He said: *"For the time will come when people will not endure sound teaching, but having itching ears they will accumulate for themselves teachers to suit their own likings, and will turn away from listening to the truth and wander into myths. As for you, always be steady, endure suffering, do the work of an evangelist, fulfill your ministry."* [3]

---

[1] 1 Th. 5:4-8.
[2] 2 Pt. 2:1-3.
[3] 2 Tim. 4:3-5.

A good example of this is the parent-child relationship. As our children mature, they challenge our training, sometimes our beliefs, and many of our rules. When we try to reason with them, they hurl back at us, "But *everybody* is doing it!" We respond, "That does *not* make it right!" This same spirit of false independence and disobedience is happening among adult Catholics. Even if *everybody* is divorced and remarried outside the Church; even if they use contraceptives; even if they "sleep together"; even if they get drunk every weekend at college; even if they have an abortion; even if they cheat their employer or on tests, that does *not* make it right.

"Revelation teaches that the power to decide what is good and what is evil does not belong to man but to God alone,"[4] John Paul II told us in *The Splendor of Truth*.

If we are seriously trying to live according to the will of God, we will faithfully follow the natural law, which is articulated in the Ten Commandments, and obey the laws and the moral teachings of the Church. Furthermore, we will make an effort to select a confessor for guidance who is faithful to the Magisterium of the Catholic Church. John Paul II adds: "...the unity of the Church is damaged not only by Christians who reject or distort the truths of faith but also by those who disregard the moral obligations to which they are called by the Gospel."[5]

Before we begin the next section, a word of caution. What follows in this chapter and in the next two chapters may appear negative or even harsh. This is not my intent. As Pope Paul VI pointed out, the greatest sin of the 20th century is the loss of the sense of sin. This "spiritual disease" has so permeated our culture and society that many people actually do not know that certain thoughts, words, actions, and omissions can be sinful. Without this knowledge, it is difficult, if not impossible, to grow in holiness. For this reason I have decided to discuss in depth the topic of sin, how we can sin, specific sins, and the degree of gravity of sins. Think of these chapters as college theology classes rather than a personal affront. In grade school it was not only interesting but such fun to ask "Father" questions

---

[4]*The Splendor of Truth*, op.cit., n.35.
[5]Ibid, n.26.

about our faith. One time a classmate asked, "If I'm ship-wrecked on an island on Sunday, is it a mortal sin if I can't get to Mass?" That question stimulated an explosion of "what ifs." Think of these chapters in that manner—as answers to questions you may have wondered about. Then take this knowledge and apply what you need to your own interior life.

How Do We Sin?

We sin by any willful *thought, desire, word, action,* or *omission* forbidden by the law of God.

Thoughts: We can offend God in our thoughts through hatred, envy, jealousy, rash judgment, impure thoughts, a longing to do something evil, approval of an evil committed by oneself or others, or a deliberate pleasure in some object presented to our imagination such as a fellow worker being fired.

Desires: We can sin in our desires through envy, jealousy, greed, lust, gluttony, desiring evil to befall another.

Words: We can sin with our words through gossip, lies, slander, back-biting, disclosing secrets or confidential information, immodest jokes, angry words.

Actions: We sin through actions opposed to the Ten Commandments, the spiritual and corporal works of mercy, the six commandments of the Church, the Christian virtues, the duties of our state of life. This will be discussed further in Chapter 6.

Omission: Sins of omission are those sins that we commit when we neglect to do our duty in regard to the spiritual and corporal works of mercy, the laws of the Church, the Christian virtues, and our state in life. For example, if we delegate the teaching of our Catholic faith to the local Catholic school or C.C.D. program but do not follow up to see what our children are learning or *if* they are learning, this could be a sin of omission since we are the primary educators of our children.[6] Pope John Paul II explains in his Apostolic Exhortation, *The Role of the Christian Family in the Modern World*, that "Sex Education, which is a basic

---

[6]Paul VI, *Declaration on Christian Education*, (Boston: St. Paul Editions, 1965), p. 8.

right and duty of parents, must always be carried out under their attentive guidance, whether at home or in educational centers chosen and controlled by them."[7] To reiterate this point, the Pontifical Council for the Family released *The Truth and Meaning of Human Sexuality*, Dec. 9th, 1995. In Part IV of this document parents are told that they are the "original and primary," "irreplaceable" educators of their children, rights which are "incapable of being entirely delegated to others or usurped by others. If, in fact, parents do not give adequate formation in chastity, they are failing in their precise duty. Likewise, they would also be guilty were they to tolerate immoral or inadequate formation being given to their children outside the home." Parents are to seek "laws that prevent and eliminate the exploitation of the sensitivity of children and adolescents" via sex education programs designed to break down natural modesty. Parents are responsible for teaching the delicate subject of sex education, chastity and modesty. When we abrogate this responsibility by turning it over to the schools without checking the content and morality of their programs and teachers we commit a serious sin of omission.

Should we fail to defend the Church when it is attacked (for example in the media) or fail to work for moral and upright laws (such as against abortion which John Paul II calls a "blight on our country") these are sins of omission. If we neglect to financially support our parish and the Church as a whole, we are committing a sin of omission.

---

[7]John Paul II, *Familiaris Consortio* (Boston: St. Paul Editions, 1981), p.61. Other sources include *Educational Guidance in Human Love* from the Sacred Congregation for Catholic Education (Boston: St. Paul Books & Media, 1983), pp.19-20, pp. 26-27, pp. 54-55; Sacred Congregation for the Doctrine of the Faith ordered published by Pope Paul VI, *Declaration on Certain Questions Concerning Sexual Ethics* (St. Paul, MN: The Wanderer Press, 1975), p. 18; Pope Pius XI, *On Christian Marriage* (New York: Paulist Press, 1941), pp. 8-9; John Paul II, Apostolic Exhortation *Catechesi Tradendae* (Boston: St. Paul Editions, 1979), p. 14, p. 57; Paul VI, *Declaration on Christian Education*, (Boston: St. Paul Editions, 1965), p.8.

The Seven Capital Sins

Original sin left our passions disordered so we tend to easily succumb to personal sin. The chief causes of our personal sins are known as the capital sins. From these sins, all others spring. Capital sins include pride, greed, lust, gluttony, envy, anger, and sloth. Each of us is tempted by these inclinations in some way. If we control our passions, we develop virtues, but if we let our passions control us, we develop vices. By examining ourselves in regard to the capital sins, we can root out these vices through prayer, by being watchful and energetic in controlling our passions. By knowing our weaknesses and temptations we can avoid situations that could lead us to sin. It is also important to control our imagination and memory. St. Teresa of Ávila said that our imagination is the mad woman of the household.

Pride is actually the origin of all sin. Remember the Garden of Eden! It is the love of self. We call it being self-centered. It is a sin that stands out like a neon sign when we interact with people. One way in which we can check to see if pride is a main problem is to monitor our conversations. Did I do all the talking? Did I ask the other person questions about their family, profession, and interests? How much did I learn about the other person from the conversation? Controlling our obsession to talk about ourselves is one thing we can take to confession. People who deal with us will be grateful!

Pride also makes us overestimate our worth. It ignores the fact that everything we possess including our talents, charm, and physical beauty comes from God. A proud person seeks constant compliments, is touchy, boastful, easily offended, holds resentments, quarrels over trifles, presumes to sit in judgment over everyone and everything, is shocked by small faults in others but blind to his or her own faults.

Vices Associated With Pride

Vices allied to pride include presumption, boasting, ambition, vanity, ostentation, and hypocrisy.

We are guilty of *presumption* when we act above our capacity, refuse to accept counsel or advice, or expose ourselves to sin or temptation.

Boasting is praising oneself, family members, race, nationality, ancestors. We see this on bumper stickers that read, "I have an honor student at _____ school." It's common to hear people boast about possessions, wealth, raises, trips, children with superior intellect, talent, or athletic ability. People also boast about charitable deeds and good works. Some even boast of their sins. Personal pride is important to us on life's journey but when it gets out of control, it becomes boasting.

We sin in regard to *ambition* when we want to be glorified by people, to dominate others, to be popular or hold positions of prestige and power. Ambition makes us haughty and intolerant of others. When consumed by it, we can defraud investors, stockholders, banks, employers, and investment houses. *The Wall Street Journal* regularly carries articles of financial misdeeds traceable to ambition. It leads not only to vanity but also business, financial, political, or personal intrigues.

Vanity is the striving after the esteem of the world. We are vain when we want others to honor and flatter us. When we are self-satisfied with ourselves and our qualities, we are vain. We are vain when we think we are pretty good people. Vanity can involve our physical looks or ability, clothing, jewelry, talents, and possessions. The vain person wants to be noticed by the upper crust of society but will not bother with the lowly, the crude or the poor. Vanity needs compliments and is disappointed when not fussed over or praised.

Ostentation is the sin of putting oneself on display or acting pompous. Besides showing off one's possessions such as diamonds, cars, summer homes, etc., the ostentatious person wants his or her good works seen by others. People may build a huge house just for ostentation and then not be able to afford furniture to fill it. One such couple I know lost their jobs. To avoid the embarrassment, they relocated to another state, bought a huge mansion and drive a new BMW to keep up appearances while they job hunt. They are still job hunting after several years. This sin can also prevent someone from taking a lower paying or less prestigious job when laid off.

Hypocrisy garbs oneself in the pretense of the virtue of humility. It is actually the excess of pride. The person may be too slothful to strive after virtue, but so thirsty for vainglory that he pretends virtue. The person does good things only when seen. He tells lies to escape blame or to seek praise.

Pride and its stepsisters have their tentacles in each of us. Pride is so strong that we are told that it will die a half an hour after we do! While we may personally have difficulty seeing it in our lives, those around us have great vantage points. Once I was part of a conversation where a woman asked a spiritual director what her major defect was. The spiritual director indicated this was not the place to discuss something like that, but the woman persisted. Finally the director indicated pride. The woman was insulted. "I may be guilty of many things, but pride is not one of them!"

We fight pride by recalling that all that we have comes from God. Meditate on the fact that we are dust and will return to dust. Without God's goodness and help we are incapable of doing anything good or even useful. If God has gifted us or our children with many talents, are these talents being used for His honor and glory? Remember we will have to account for them when we stand before God. Rather than being smug about our successes, we should be concerned with our intentions. Do we offer our work and talents to God? Is our work done for the honor and glory of God or to further our ambitions? St. Alphonsus Maria De Liguori teaches: "It is not enough to do good works; they need to be done well. For our works to be good and perfect, they must be done for the sole purpose of pleasing God." If we have authority over others, it is given to us by God, it is not because these people are beneath us. Use all authority with charity, compassion, and with a spirit of service. When tempted to exaggerate, remember that God knows the truth. If tempted by intolerance, remember that God puts up with our nonsense. For those moments of vanity, we can remind ourselves that sickness or an accident can disfigure our face or body. Earthly honor can end any moment with our death.

What's Avarice?

Avarice or greed is disorderly covetousness and is also present in every sin. It is the disordered love of money or earthly goods. Today it is called materialism. Before Lee Atwater, the chairman of the Republican National Committee, died in 1991, he said, "The '80's were about acquiring—acquiring wealth, power, prestige. I know. I acquired more wealth, power and prestige than most. But you can acquire all you want and still feel empty...It took a deadly illness to put me eye to eye with truth, but it is a truth that the country, caught up in ruthless ambitions and moral decay, can learn on my dime."[8]

Luxury is also part of this vice. It is the passion or drive to possess the newest items out or the top of the line of consumer items. It is the excess of spending. By being frugal, avoiding impulse buying, and consulting a spiritual director about expensive purchases, we can avoid falling into the trap (and the lap) of luxury.

Connected sins are *miserliness* and *niggardliness (stinginess)*. These two sins seek to increase savings or possessions through petty savings. We are miserly when we are stingy with ourselves. We are niggardly when we stint others. Polls in newspapers indicate that of all denominations, Catholics donate the *least amount of money* to their Church. This is niggardliness on our part. When avaricious, we are hardhearted and pitiless toward others. We want to hold on to all we have. We will spend on ourselves but close our eyes to the needs of those around us. It eats away at our faith while alienating us from the love of God and neighbor. Remember, the desire of money is the root of all evil.[9] The pursuit of money or possessions can become our "golden calf." We may even plunk our children into daycare so we can buy a bigger house or go on nicer vacations. We can seek wealth to the detriment of our own health (the workaholics) or to the detriment of our employees' health and safety. As employers do we pay our employees a just wage? Do we pay our bills on time? Do we donate our time and money to the poor and helpless? One Christmas a wealthy family spent a day together baking cookies for a welfare family. The wife still brags about this "work of charity." It was not charity for that family. The welfare family needed food and clothing, not daintily decorated cookies!

Morbid curiosity is part of avarice. Having to listen, watch, or read the latest news, scandals, or other information can be

---

[8]"Ranting, Raving Not Populism," by John Tiffany in *The Spotlight* (Washington, DC) Aug. 21, 1995, p.7.
[9]1 Timothy 6,10.

detrimental to our spiritual, moral, and physical well-being. It also makes us less fruitful. We cannot watch TV or read such materials and still do our daily duties and good works. Morbid curiosity can disturb our consciences and peace of mind. The desire to know the future leads to the occult, divination, witchcraft, tarot cards, and the use of psychics.

What About Envy?

Envy is sadness over the good fortune of others such as their talents, wealth, possessions, and successes. This sin comes from pride and covetousness. When we envy, we belittle another's esteem. *Jealousy* is fear that another will take something from us. These sins are vices opposed to charity. In addition, envy and jealousy stir up hatred. It leads to speaking ill of others, to backbiting, ridiculing, unfairness, injustice, persecution, and discord. It causes the breakup of friendships and the removal from jobs of competent people. In addition, it causes vengeance and wars. To combat this common sin, we should try to detach ourselves from the world and think about eternity. Besides speaking well of those you envy, pray for them, render them services, defend them before others. Charity can overcome envy and jealousy.

The Sin of Anger

Anger is the disorderly desire for retribution for an injury that is real or imagined. Anger forces us to vent our feelings. It is visible in the color or expression on our face and in our gestures. Anger can grow into *violence* or *fury*. Anger makes us lose our temper. It darkens our intellect so that we are blinded to the rights of others. This sin exhausts our strength and shortens our lives, besides causing us mental and physical anguish. It can also cause health problems. There is no peace nor happiness around a person filled with anger. An angry person becomes an enemy of God.

Related sins include *quarrels, discord, insults, gossip, slander, revealing secrets, spite, ill will, resentment, hatred, and revenge*. Talebearing is gossiping, or telling what one person said against another. The motive for talebearing is usually pride or envy and leads to rash judgment, enmity, vengeance, revenge, and disunity. Try to refrain from speaking when angry or from engaging in conversations that can inflame anger. Reflect on all the suffering brought about by anger. Foster kind and forgiving thoughts toward the offending people. Pray and learn to forgive. In regard to slander, gossip, and secrets, we certainly do not want to be messengers of evil, so if we cannot say anything good about a person, it's best to refrain from speaking.

What Exactly Is Lust?

Lust is the disorderly desire for pleasure in our thoughts, words, desires, and actions. Many people today mistake lust for love. Lust leads to the sins of *contraception, fornication (pre-marital sex), immodesty in dress or speech, adultery, incest, criminal assault, rape, homosexuality, sacrilege, masturbation, impure touches, immodest reading and looks, and pornography.* These sins can lead to many kinds of disorders. To avoid them, we must cultivate the virtue of purity and avoid near occasions of sin such as risqué movies and plays, language, conversation, books, and companions. Avoid soap operas and TV talk shows that promote the tearing down of morality in our culture. As Sen. Joseph Lieberman (D-Conn) told the Senate, talk shows are promoting the abnormal as normal. [10] Not only are they destroying our culture, they are presenting immorality as the norm. In addition, we should avoid idleness by keeping busy by doing something worthwhile.

It is also prudent to avoid undo familiarity with the opposite sex. Company dinners or sports teams should include spouses. Married couples have to prudently protect their marital love by avoiding business trips with a member of the opposite sex. Lengthy travel time together, in addition to staying at the same hotel can place both parties in an occasion of sin. After business hours, over a leisurely dinner at the hotel along with a couple of drinks, infatuation and affairs can develop. Long business trips or vacations without our spouse can not only lead to temptation, but also can result in the destruction of marriages. For example, a couple of months ago a young wife and mother felt compelled to get away on a cruise. Her husband did not want to go along so she went with a group of friends. On the cruise a handsome, foreign waiter catered to her every whim, providing the attention her husband should have given her. When the cruise ended, Jill and the waiter corresponded. Within a matter of weeks she

---

[10]Oct. 30, 1995.

told her stunned husband that she wanted a divorce. In the same week that I heard about this, a friend called to tell me that her marriage is breaking up because her husband has a mistress in a foreign country.

The Sin Of Gluttony

Gluttony is the inordinate use of food or drink. (Blessed Josemaría warns, "Gluttony is the forerunner of impurity."[11]) Related sins are *bulimia* and *drunkenness*. Americans have the reputation of always having food or drink in our hands. One bishop visiting from Rome remarked that he was shocked by all the obese people he saw in the US. He commented, "These obese people flock to fast food outlets and buffets like flies!" Overeating leads to *laziness, sensuality*, and *sloth* and damages our health. Gluttony, which fosters immoderation, weakens our will. We should eat to live, not live to eat. We should also be careful not to eat so much that it makes our mind sluggish and our waist lines increase. It is better to eat less than more. We should say grace before meals, eat at set times, and abstain from eating between meals. This strengthens our wills. Also, we should be aware of nervous eating. My husband works at a hospital that is preparing to undergo its regular review. Tensions began building toward the end of the preparation period. Suddenly he noticed that every woman coming into his office to sign documents or to resolve a problem brought along food. They are all nervous eaters. Rather than depending on food to help us through tough spots, we should rely on God and prayer.

Drunkenness leads to the loss of reason and excites one to *lust, anger, quarreling*, and of course, leads to ill health. Dating and drinking lead to the loss of reserve and modesty, besides being the common cause of the loss of virginity. There is a correlation between drunkenness and the growing abortion and illegitimacy rates.

To illustrate this, one day a young woman stopped by our house to pick up an audio tape. Although a stranger, she asked to talk to me. She told me she was pregnant and was considering an abortion. Peggy wanted to discuss her options. When I recovered my composure, Peggy explained that she had "gone

---

[11]*The Way*, op. cit., #126.

out drinking with some friends." She was picked up by a fellow whose name she did not even know. She was drunk and she fell for his lines. They had relations in his car in the parking lot of the bar. Now she was pregnant. As shocking as her story is, Peggy disclosed this was the *second* time this had happened to her. Since my experience with Peggy, I have learned that this scenario is being tragically repeated by thousands of young women. Drinking and dating are a dangerous combination. To combat these tendencies, we should consider not drinking on dates or at mixed parties, *especially* on college campuses. The other obvious way to prevent drunkenness is moderation in drinking. Decide before going out that you will have only one drink and then stick to it. It is a serious sin to drive under the influence of alcohol because it not only endangers your life but also the lives of others.

Sloth

Sloth is sluggishness of mind, body, and soul. It causes us to dislike bodily exertion making us apathetic to action. Sloth is the disease of the will that fears effort and hardship. It inclines us to avoid labor and seek unneeded rest. Work becomes too burdensome. Related sins are *idleness,* laziness, and *fraud* toward employers.

Many people feign work related injuries so they do not have to work. They may even take a business to court to get long term payments to avoid having to return to work. This is gravely wrong and sinful. When we take long lunches, chat for long times on personal calls, or wander the halls to chat with friends and other employees, we are being slothful and defrauding our employers. If we prefer only to watch TV or read novels rather than cleaning our homes and making good meals for our families we are slothful. When people ask for our help but we decline out of laziness, we are slothful. If we are not concerned enough to learn the views of the political candidates and work for honest ones, we are slothful. By being slothful in regard to the political process, we allow immoral laws to be enacted. Sloth is a grievous sin when it deals with the duties of our state in life.

To counter the tendency to be slothful, we can rest from one type of work by doing another. If we strive to do each of our duties completely, punctually, and with perfection, our wills become strengthen so we can fight slothful temptations.

We can also be spiritually slothful. Sloth of the soul is called *lukewarmness*. Lukewarmness encourages us to shorten or omit our religious duties and prayers. Sloth becomes a mortal sin if it affects our spiritual life to the injury of our soul. When we do not dedicate enough time each day to personal prayer—no matter how busy we are—we are slothful. By developing a schedule that includes prayer, spiritual reading, daily Mass (when possible), the rosary, and frequent confession, we can avoid spiritual sloth.

This listing of capital sins is meant to educate us, not discourage us. Once we can identify areas in which we need to improve, we can then work toward acquiring virtues and eliminating vice, good habits instead of bad habits. The *Catholic Catechism* tells us that moral virtues grow through education, deliberate acts, and perseverance in our daily struggle. In addition, God's infinite graces constantly elevate and purify our actions.

Virtue is truly its own reward. A person guided by moral principles and who is struggling to grow in virtue while fighting the above vices is more consistent and reliable. The virtuous person lives according to duties and principles, and strives to do what is right in all situations. As a result, he enjoys peace of conscience and the respect of all who deal with him.[12]

Saint Maximilian Kolbe explains: "Everyone around us has the right to demand and desire of us good example. He who does not give good example sins not only against God, but in the presence of all his neighbors. Therefore he is the occasion of another's sins."

"My son, where do men find in you the Christ they are looking for? In your pride? In your desire to impose yourself on others? In those little character defects which you don't wish to overcome? In your stubbornness?...Is Christ to be found there? No, he is not!" writes Blessed Josemaría.

"You need to have your own personality, agreed. But you should try to make it conform exactly to Christ's."[13]

---

[12]Material taken from audio tapes based on the book *Know Yourself* by Joseph Malaise, SJ.
[13]*The Forge*, op. cit., #468.,

CHAPTER 5

Let's Not Be Naive

"Mortal sin is very rare; only depraved and very evil people commit mortal sins. Thus there is no need to go to confession."

With the promotion of the philosophy of "if it feels good, do it," sin and its effects are very widespread—and growing—in our global community. Sin is saying "no" to God and that scream of "no" loudly resounds throughout the world. In the approved apparitions of Our Lady in Kibeho, Rwanda, Africa in 1983, she told the visionary Anathalie: "Sins are more numerous than drops of water in the sea."[1] Our sins made Christ sweat blood in the Garden of Olives. Our sins were responsible for His dreadful scourging and His horrifying crowning with thorns. If these sufferings weren't enough, our sins were the cause of His gruesome death on the Cross. If we would take the time to meditate on this we could begin to see the seriousness of each sin. Why then are people today so casual in disregarding the tremendous seriousness of sin? Is it because we have moved so far away from God that our consciences have lost sensitivity toward good and evil? It is a fact that the closer we are to God, the more careful we will be not to offend Him even with "little white lies." The farther away we are from God, the more likely we will be living in the state of mortal sin.

---

[1]"Bishop Gehanany of Kibeho states he has approved these apparitions in the first stage. Thomas W. Petrisko, *Call of the Ages* (Santa Barbara, CA: Queenship, 1995), p.18. Approval given Aug. 15, 1988.

A mortal sin completely cuts us off from God. Should we die in the state of mortal sin, we will spend eternity in Hell. A venial sin, until it is fully repented or atoned for, cuts us off from the full possession of God's Beatific Vision. That is why Purgatory exists.

John Paul II addressed the issue of sin during his homily in San Antonio, Texas in 1987: "In different parts of the world there is *a great neglect of the Sacrament of Penance.* This is sometimes linked to an obscuring of the religious and moral conscience, a loss of the sense of sin, or a lack of adequate instruction on the importance of this Sacrament in the life of Christ's Church. At times the neglect occurs because we fail to take seriously our lack of love and justice, and God's corresponding offer of reconciling mercy. Sometimes there is a hesitation or an unwillingness to accept maturely and responsibly the consequences of the objective truths of faith."

While there is a casual attitude about sin in general, venial sins are simply dismissed as of no consequence or the product of human nature. The saints disagree. In a vision, St. Teresa of Ávila saw the place reserved for her in Hell if she had not changed her lifestyle. Her venial sins would have gradually led to mortal sins. St. Catherine of Siena fainted at the vision of a hideous soul deformed by venial sin. Mary, the sister of Moses, murmured against him and was punished with leprosy. After wandering in the desert for 40 years, enduring the treachery and the whining of the Israelites, Moses was denied entry into the promised land for *momentarily* doubting God. Likewise, Zachary was struck deaf and dumb when he doubted the message of the angel.

Venial sins *are* serious concerns. Bishop Vaughan remarks, "How different things would be in these days, if every uncharitable thought and every unkind word were to engender, as soon as uttered, some very painful and loathsome disease which would rack our nerves with pain! But such is not God's method. His punishment for venial sin is far worse than any leprosy, but he reserves it for another world. We shall understand something of the evil of venial sin when we are burning amid the purging flames of Purgatory."[2] Remember, *every* sin we commit, even

---

[2]Bishop John S. Vaughan, *Venial Sin* (London, England: Westminster, 1923), p. 18.

when it is forgiven, must be atoned for in some way, either in this life or in Purgatory. Purgatory is a painful reality. For those interested, read the little stories that accompany the Novena to the Holy Souls. Those stories beat anything written by Edgar Allan Poe.

Cardinal A. Gasquet, OSB, writes: "It is to be feared that there are not a few amongst us who flippantly declare that, whilst of course they desire to keep themselves free from any grievous offense against God, they have no particular desire to be saints, by which they mean that they regard the avoidance of every small sin as almost impossible to the ordinary man, and as only to be looked for in those whom God has called to walk in the higher paths of perfection. This notion shows how little such people remember that God has called every soul He has created to be holy—that is, to be pure and free from the stain of even small blemishes in His sight, and that every offense against His law is an evil thing which must be avoided at all cost."[3]

What Is A Venial Sin?

Personal sin falls into two categories: venial sin or mortal sin (C.C. 1854-1856).

A *venial sin* is an offense against God that does not deprive our souls of sanctifying grace. Should we die with only venial sins on our souls we would go to Purgatory. A sin can be venial when the evil done is not seriously wrong or when the evil done is seriously wrong, but the sinner sincerely believes it is only slightly wrong, or does not give full consent to it. A "white lie" is a venial sin because it is not seriously wrong. Refusing to speak or associate with a friend or family member is seriously wrong but we may not realize the gravity of what we are doing. Therefore, it is a venial sin. On the other hand, we may realize that not speaking is wrong, but each time we attempt to heal the rupture, the person is not open to us or we lack the courage to mend the rift. We are then not giving our full consent to the sin.

Many people have the mistaken idea that venial sins are not something to avoid or to be concerned about, yet they can hamper our spiritual growth. We give in easier to temptations. "Venial sin also increases the violence and the strength of our spiri-

---

[3]Ibid, p.1.

tual enemies, by which I mean our passions, sinful desires, and evil inclinations."[4] Venial sin chips away at our devotion. We become spiritually lazy and lukewarm. (Remember God vomits the lukewarm.[5] That's pretty strong!) Prayers are skipped. Our reverence in church and before the Blessed Sacrament becomes casual, as well as our dress. It becomes difficult to do spiritual reading, go on retreat, fight our vices and imperfections. Venial sin weakens our soul and intensifies our love of pleasure. Soccer games or golfing become more important than daily Mass or even Sunday Mass. TV or videos replace the family rosary. The work of the Holy Spirit is obstructed in our souls. Not only that, venial sin weakens our wills. We become reluctant to do works of charity or works of service for family or neighbor. Our vices strengthen so that it is easier for us to fall into mortal sin. "Small sins pave the way for more serious ones....No one becomes wicked all at once."[6] We become evil little by little.

St. Gregory contends that venial sins are dangerous because they make less of an impression on us so we commit them thoughtlessly and frequently. The more frequently we commit the same sin, the more it becomes an ingrained habit, a vice. For instance, it is so common today to hear people take the holy name of Jesus in vain or even God's name dropped into casual conversation. This is a vice easily picked up from TV shows, videos, books, and the example of family members or friends. By bowing our heads on hearing the holy name and saying a prayer in reparation, we can fortify ourselves against falling into the same vice.

Venerable Louis of Granada reminds us, "I pray you then to do all in your power to avoid these sins, for there is no enemy too weak to harm us if we make no resistance. Slight anger, gluttony, vanity, idle words and thoughts, immoderate laughter, loss of time, too much sleeping, trivial lies or flatteries—such are the sins against which I would particularly warn you. Great vigilance is required against offenses of this kind, for occasions of venial sin abound."[7]

---

[4]Ibid, p.27.

[5]Rev. 3:16.

[6]Ibid, p.26

[7]Venerable Louis of Granada, *The Sinner's Guide* (Rockford, IL: Tan Books and Publishers, Inc., 1985), p. 312.

The above is just the tip of the venial sin iceberg. Bishop John Vaughan gives another list of venial sins worth examining ourselves on: "They misjudge their neighbors, they entertain uncharitable thoughts; or they are testy, jealous, and exacting. They say their prayers in a distracted, inattentive, perfunctory manner. Perhaps they are easily ruffled, and have a few angry words with their wives or children. They allow little things to put them out. They murmur and scold because dinner is not properly cooked, or because the soup is cold. Or they give way to irritation because they are kept waiting at the door, or because their call has not been returned, or their pressing business letter has received no answer, or because they imagine that they have been, in some way, slighted or treated with scant courtesy and respect. Then on occasion they will tell what are called 'white lies,' and repeat ill-natured tales, just to amuse their neighbors.

"In short, in these and in a thousand other small ways they fall short of absolute perfection; so that day after day the impalpable dust of sins falls and gathers about their souls."[8]

The seriousness of venial sins is often obscured by the even greater evil surrounding us. This however does not lessen the impact of venial sins.

To emphasize the gravity of venial sins, Fr. Federico Suarez writes, "The mystery of iniquity, sin, is something very real and very serious. So much so, that if one single sin could prevent a war (with all the suffering that means for innocent parties), if one single sin could wipe out hunger and thirst, and pain, and physical death, it still would not be licit to commit it. Sin is worse than all the evils it gives rise to."[9]

The Cur of Ars believed, "If you really love God, you will not be content with avoiding big sins. You will regard as hateful anything which could be even a little displeasing to him."[10]

Blessed Josemaría Escrivá counsels, "Ask the Lord to grant you all the sensitivity you need to realize how evil venial sin is,

---

[8]*Venial Sin*, op. cit., p. 7.
[9] Frederico Suarez, *Penance* (New Rochelle, NY: Scepter, 1987), p. 20.
[10] *Ibid.*, p. 61.

so as to recognise it as an outright and fundamental enemy of your soul, and, with God's grace, to avoid it."[11]

What Is Mortal Sin?

A *mortal sin*, on the other hand, is a much graver offense against God. In *The Splendor Of Truth*, the Holy Father quotes from the Council of Trent: "...[M]ortal sin is sin whose object is grave matter and which is also committed with full knowledge and deliberate consent." He continues: "With the whole tradition of the Church, we call mortal sin the act by which man freely and consciously rejects God, His law, the covenant of love that God offers, preferring to turn in on himself or to some created and finite reality, something contrary to the divine will. This can occur in a direct and formal way, in the sins of idolatry, apostasy and atheism; or in an equivalent way, as in every act of disobedience to God's commandments in a grave matter."[12]

Mortal sin separates us from God by destroying sanctifying grace (God's life) in our souls. Mortal sin kills our interior life. In other words, mortal sin causes *spiritual death*. We lose all supernatural merit for any good actions that we do while in the state of mortal sin. In addition, we allow ourselves to be manipulated by the tyrannical rule of Satan. Our natural inclination towards virtue is weakened. The sinner becomes more inclined to sin and less inclined to what is good....Passions become stronger and the power of the will weaker, debilitating even further the harmony that should exist between intellect, will and appetites. Mortal sin removes our interior peace. Suddenly there is inner conflict, remorse, unrest, discontentment, and turmoil. One cannot kill the life of God within and still maintain interior peace and joy. Eventually mortal sin can even cause mental and physical illnesses. The final effect of mortal sin is the separation of the sinner from his fellow Christians and mankind in general. Should we die in the state of mortal sin, we would spend eternity in Hell. To chose to commit a mortal sin is a *deadly* decision.

Let's digress for a moment to consider the topic of Hell. Today, along with the loss of the sense of sin, there is a denial

---

[11]Blessed Josemaría Escrivá, *The Forge* (New York: Scepter Press, 1988), #114

[12]*The Splendor of Truth*, op.cit. n.70.

of Hell. While we should fear committing a mortal sin because it is such a great offense against the God we love, our fallen nature may not always grasp this truth. Fear of Hell can keep us on the path to Heaven. Although many people deny the reality of Hell, it *does* exist. In the Old Testament there are over thirty references to it. In the New Testament, Jesus speaks more of Hell than of Heaven. In fact, He even tells a parable about Hell (Luke 16:19-31). Besides saints and visionaries who were taken to Hell, there are numerous stories told and written about it. Even my mother tells a story about my grandaunt who was married to an atheist. When his family tried to convert him, he just laughed. He so scorned the thought of an afterlife that he told them that if there was one, he would come back to let them know. After he died, my aunt was having dinner with his family one evening. The discussion turned to "Pa" and eternity. One of his children remarked, "Guess, there's no afterlife 'cause Pa never came back." Suddenly a ball of flame rolled down the dining room table, then disappeared. All present were confirmed in their belief of an afterlife!

In 1917, Our Lady showed the children of Fatima Hell. Lucia, one of the children writes: "...[W]e saw as it were a sea of fire. Plunged in this fire were demons and souls in human form, like transparent burning embers, all blackened or burnished bronze, floating about in the conflagration, now raised into the air by the flames that issued from within themselves together with great clouds of smoke, now falling back on every side like sparks in huge fires, without weight or equilibrium, amid shrieks and groans of pain and despair, which horrified us and made us tremble with fear....[W]e looked up at Our Lady, who said to us so sadly: *'You have seen Hell where the souls of poor sinners go....'*" During another apparition Our Lady also told the children, *"More souls go to Hell because of sins of the flesh than for any other reason."*

Blessed Faustina wrote in 1936: "Today, I was led by an angel to the chasms of Hell. It is a place of great torture....[T]he first torture that constitutes Hell is the loss of God; the second is perpetual remorse of conscience; the third is that one's condition will never change; the forth is the fire that will penetrate the soul without destroying it—a terrible suffering, since it is a purely spiritual fire, lit by God's anger; the fifth torture is continual darkness and a terrible suffocating smell, and, despite the darkness, the devils and the souls of the damned see each other and all the evil, both of others and their own; the sixth torture is the constant company of Satan; the seventh torture is the horrible despair, hatred of God, vile words, curses and blasphemies...There are special tortures destined for particular souls. These are the torments of the senses. Each soul undergoes terrible and indescribable sufferings, related to the manner in which it has sinned...Let the sinner know that he will be tortured throughout all eternity, in those senses which he made use of to sin. I am writing this at the command of God, so that no soul may find an excuse by saying there is no Hell, or that nobody has ever been there, and so no one can say what it is like."[13]

Despite the existence of Hell, many people today prefer to sin and presume the mercy of God. God is merciful, but He is also just. Would it be just of God to treat those who obey His laws and commands despite hardship and suffering the same as those who disobeyed Him?

Let's look at this another way. Sometimes we are like stubborn children. We know deep down in our hearts what is best for us but we refuse to follow the law of God. By leading a life opposed to the will of God, we condemn ourselves to Hell. *God does not condemn us. Our life condemns us.* Even if God continued to offer to us eternal life, our pride and stubbornness would continue to refuse God's offer just as we did on earth.

Keeping the reality of Hell in mind, let's return to the topic of mortal sin.

What Makes A Sin Mortal?

How do we know when a sin is mortal? To be a mortal sin, it must involve a grave matter, we must give the matter sufficient reflection, and our full consent (C.C. 1857-1861). All three conditions must be present in order for a sin to be mortal. While a certain sin can be mortal, ignorance, fear, anger, compulsion, depression, nervous diseases or other strong emotions

---

[13]Blessed Faustina Kowalska, *Divine Mercy in My Soul*, The Diary of Sister M. Faustina Kowalska (Stockbridge, MA: Marian Press, 1987), #741 (#160-161).

can lessen responsibility for the action. So as we go through the rest of this chapter, let us keep this fact in mind. We can judge the sin but never the sinner because only God knows the heart and will of each person. Now for some examples. If a couple uses contraception in ignorance, it is not a mortal sin for them. A high school girl may be violently threatened by her parents if she does not have an abortion. Fear and the lack of her full consent mitigate the seriousness of her action. A person who gossips but thinks he or she is merely entertaining people lacks sufficient reflection. Teens who commit impure acts on dates may never have been taught the moral seriousness of these acts. As we grow in our faith, sometimes we realize the seriousness of our past actions. Rather than becoming scrupulous over the past, we have to remember that sins committed in our past lives due to ignorance, lack of sufficient reflection and the absence of full consent are not mortal sins.

On the other hand, when all three conditions are present— grave matter, sufficient reflection and full consent, a thought, word, action or omission becomes a mortal sin.

Does this mean that if a man and a woman live together without benefit of marriage they commit a mortal sin? Yes. If I get deliberately drunk am I committing a mortal sin? Yes. What if I don't go to Sunday Mass while on vacation? Is that a mortal sin? Yes, if Mass is missed deliberately.

St. Paul gives another list of mortal sins. He speaks against "immorality, uncleanness, licentiousness, idolatry, witchcraft, enmities, contention, jealousies, anger, quarrels, factions, sects, envies, murders, drunkenness, carousing and such like...they who do such things will not attain the kingdom of Heaven."[14] This is a list that fits our own times as well.

John Paul II lists other mortal sins: "Whatever is hostile to life itself, such as any kind of homicide, genocide, abortion, euthanasia and voluntary suicide; whatever violates the integrity of the human person, such as mutilation, physical and mental torture and attempts to coerce the spirit; whatever is offensive to human dignity, such as subhuman living conditions, arbitrary imprisonment, deportation, slavery, prostitution and trafficking

---

[14]Gal. 6:19-22.

in women and children; degrading conditions of work which treat laborers as mere instruments of profit, and not as free responsible persons."[15]

While we may consider ourselves good people, if we are *not* in the state of grace because of mortal sin, we may be nice people but we are not good people.

Can you find a single family not touched in some way by one of its members or an extended family member living in the state of mortal sin? No one seems to be shocked or scandalize by this state of "affairs." Newspapers, magazines, books, and TV are filled with mortal sin and its euphemisms. These include "planned parenthood," "bribery," "pro-choice," "murder," "alternative lifestyle," "swindle," "living together," "armed robber," "death with dignity," "fraud," "mercy killing," "gay lifestyle," "criminal conspiracy," "RU 486," "skimming off the top," "abortion," "burglary," "genetic experimentation," "cover-up," "fetal tissue research," "hijacker," "in vitro fertilization," "perjury," "artificial insemination," "DUI," "terrorist," "surrogate mother," "bomber," "rape," "drug trafficking," "incest," "pornography," "abuse of authority," "sexual revolution," "illicit financial favors," "masturbation," "gunmen," "Norplant," "slaying," "IUD," "massacre," "cohabitation," "inmate rampage," "sex scandal," "looting," "lesbian," "rioting," "transsexual," "disinformation," "blended families" formed through "divorce and remarriage," "payoffs," "vasectomy," concealed information," "condom," "victimized another," "The Pill," etc. Not only are we surrounded by mortal sin, society is drowning in it!

There are two popular errors today that bear strongly on the deformation of consciences. They are called *Situation Ethics* and The *Fundamental Option Theory*. "*Situation Ethics* teaches that there is no fixed moral code given to human beings by the Creator. It holds that individuals must make moral choices (choices about right and wrong) according to a particular situation—that is, what is right or best in this moment for me. This false theory permits gravely sinful actions, and leads people who follow it down the road to despair because the human mind cannot long be pressured into calling gravely sinful matters 'slight.'"[16]

---

[15]*Splendor of Truth*, op. cit., n.80.
[16] *Basic Catechism*, *(Boston: Daughters of St. Paul, 1984)*, p. 136.

The *Fundamental Option Theory* has a slightly different twist. "By this abuse is meant that if a good man does something gravely sinful that particular action is not gravely sinful for him. One gravely sinful act (a mortal sin) is not enough to separate him from God; a series of gravely forbidden acts would be required. This teaching is false and is not what the Church teaches regarding sin or man's free will and personal responsibility for his actions."[17]

In the Gospel of St. Matthew, Christ tells the crowd, *"...[E]very kind of sin and blasphemy shall be forgiven men; but the blasphemy against the Spirit will not be forgiven. And whoever speaks words against the Son of Man, it shall be forgiven him; but whoever speaks against the Holy Spirit, it will not be forgiven him, either in this world or in the world to come."*[18] What are the sins against the Holy Spirit? While all sin is a turning away from God, most of the time this turning away is done through human weakness. When we turn from God out of sheer malice or deliberately refuse God's graces, we sin against the Holy Spirit. Among the sins of obstinate malice are voluntary despairing of God's power to save us, presumption of being saved without any merit on our part, resisting the truth revealed by God, voluntary sadness for the grace possessed by others, obstinacy in sin, and final impenitence. It may seem perhaps very unlikely that anyone could refuse his own salvation; but if we consider that many of our contemporaries are so closed to the very idea of God and to the redemptive will of Christ, such obstinate malice, sadly enough, does no longer seem to be so rare. Through the accumulation of selfishness, prejudice, voluntary ignorance, pride and cowardice, a man can in fact harden his heart and reject the love of God through obstinate malice. An example of this would be a member of freemasonry who not only turned from God himself, but forbade his Catholic wife Sunday Mass, the sacraments, and the Catholic education of his children.

The World, The Flesh, And The Devil

One of the greatest gifts that God gives to us is the gift of freedom. We have the ability by using our free-will to control or

---

[17] *Ibid.*, p. 136.
[18] Matt. 12:31-32.

initiate our actions. By acting or not acting, we shape our lives. Freedom can be used for growth and maturity, leading us eventually to unite our will with God's, or freedom can be used to enslave us in an endless spiral of misery if we become entrapped in a sinful lifestyle. Since we are free, we are also responsible for our actions although our freedom of action can be nullified or diminished through habit, ignorance, fear, threats, forcible restraint, oversight, social and psychological factors. Obstacles to the right use of our freedom are the world, the flesh (concupiscence) and the devil. Concupiscence is the enemy within our hearts, which the world and the devil seek to exploit. In order to better understand what we are dealing with, let's consider briefly how the flesh, the world and the devil seek to separate us from God.

Concupiscence of the flesh is the disordered love of sense-pleasure. Pleasure well ordered and directed toward our love for God is morally good. When we seek pleasure for its own sake, however, it becomes disordered. Eating is good if done to keep our bodies healthy. But when we overindulge in food and drink we live to eat, rather that eat to live. The physical love between a man and a woman is holy and pleasing to God as long as it is within marriage and allows for the generation of children. Outside of marriage and/or with the use of contraceptives in marriage, it becomes lust.

Concupiscence of the flesh is dangerous because our entire body becomes involved through the use of our senses. We tend to pamper ourselves in regard to rest, health, and our individual cravings. Sometimes our bodies and their wants become more important to us than our souls.

Concupiscence of the eyes concerns our natural curiosity and our love for the goods of this world. We all are eager to know the latest news and gossip. We long to know what is going to happen in the future rather than placing our future in God's hands and letting Him play it out. Some people devote their whole lives to acquiring worldly wisdom but have no time to get to know God Who is Wisdom itself. When we read books, see plays, or watch TV and movies without discretion, we are feeding our curiosity for worldly issues and possibly injuring our souls in the process.

Concupiscence of the eyes also covers the love of wealth, position, and power, which is better known as *avarice*. It can cause us to abandon our duties to our spouse and children in order to pursue a higher position or more wealth. When we place our hope for the future in worldly power instead of in God, we are guilty of this sin.

Pride of life is the worship of self. Sometimes we forget that we are here only because God willed our existence. Everything we have—our talents, our successes, our position, our possessions, our continued existence on earth—comes from God. We are *not* self-sufficient. If God chose to forget us, we and all we possess would cease to be.

From pride of life *egoism* flows. It is accompanied by vanity, vainglory, boasting (about our achievements and good works), ostentation (showing off our clothes, jewelry, home, possessions), and hypocrisy (pretense of virtue)...that whole list we covered in the last chapter.

When we speak about *the world* and its effect on us, we are talking about people who are hostile to religion, individuals who are hardened sinners and those who are known as worldlings. The people hostile to religion are so because religion condemns their pride, their sensuality, and their greed for material goods. The indifferent are those who do not want to be moved from their apathy toward God. Hardened sinners love sin because they love disordered pleasure and are not going to part with it. Worldlings, on the other hand, believe in God and practice their religion, but combine it with their love of pleasure and luxury. Their morals fluctuate to suit the situation. These various attitudes of the world pervade every facet of our lives. At times it's hard to follow Christ when everyone else seems to be going in the opposite direction.[19] The world also means the environment of selfishness and materialism that attracts people. We see this in the Yuppie lifestyle and the New Age Movement.

The *Devil* and his legions have the power to act upon our senses and imaginations. Fr. John A. Hardon, SJ observes: "Un-

---

[19] Adolphe Tanquerey, SS, DD,*The Spiritual Life—A Treatise On Ascetical and Mystical Theology (Belgium: Desclee & Company, 1930)*, pp. 101-115.

truth, deceit, arousing desires, and releasing the passions are the four pillars, so to speak, of the demonic methodology."[20] Satan and his cohorts coax our wills to sin. They help us to rationalize sin. They encourage us to take short cuts in our struggle for sanctity so that we become first lukewarm and then cold. They want to divert our attention from God's will to our own wills. They attract our attention to the materialism and the sensuality of the world. They constantly remind us how repugnant suffering is. They also make us feel sad or discouraged by our faults thereby tempting us to give up the battle to be good and holy people.

St. Ignatius in his *Spiritual Exercises* writes that Satan first tempts men to covet riches (materialism). Once the person is hooked on materialism, he uses man's natural desire for honors and recognition (popularity and prestige). This leads to the sin of pride. Once caught like a fly in this spider web, it is very difficult to escape.

George Huber explains, "Satan and his troops have power over the world of matter. They can play with material things the same way a child plays with marbles. Although man's mind and will are forbidden territory to them, they still have access to his external senses and lower faculties—imagination, sensibility, memory. By influencing these faculties they indirectly reach his mind and will. Just think of the role that sense-images, feelings and impulses play in a person's behavior and it is easy to realize that the devil has a great deal of scope for influencing our decisions and behavior. He can awaken sense-images and cause us to have feelings which affect our thinking and incline our will in the direction that suits him."[21]

With such influences going against us, it is clear to see how easy it is for us to slip from temptation into sin if we are not growing in grace and in the love of God.

Why do we consent to sin? Catholic author Russell Shaw claims that "It is often more convenient to turn against a human good in order to get out of a tight spot (for instance, solving a

---

[20]John A. Hardon, SJ, *Spiritual Life In The Modern World* (Boston: Daughters of St. Paul, 1982), p.35.

[21]George Huber, *My Angel will Go Before You* (Dubin, Ireland: Four Courts, 1983), p.55.

problem by cheating on an exam, using company supplies for personal use, by having an abortion, etc.). It is convenient, in other words, to sin."[22]

Following the natural law, the Ten Commandments, and the directives of the Church can cause us to come into conflict with society and the world at large that has lost the sense of sin. Yet, if we follow the ways of the world, the personal consequences are great. Still, we will never find happiness, peace, or contentment if we turn away from God. Furthermore, how can we turn from a God who loves us so dearly to the world that will despise us tomorrow?

---

[22] Russell Shaw, *Why We Need Confession* (Huntington, IN: Our Sunday Visitor, 1986), p. 56.

CHAPTER 6

A Good Confession Depends
Upon The Ten Commandments

*"God is not legalistic— so don't be concerned
about making an examination of conscience before
confession, or considering the Ten Commandments. God does not want a laundry list: the
important thing is to say what you feel."*

The Sacrament of Reconciliation is a *powerful* sacrament. The way we use it determines our address in eternity. God knows all the sins we committed since our last confession. We cannot surprise Him. But He waits in the confessional to hear if *we* will have the humility to admit them, not only to Him but also to ourselves. For this reason, it is important to prepare well for confession. This means examining our consciences by mentally going through the Ten Commandments, the Precepts of the Church, and the spiritual and corporal works of mercy. It is also helpful to read Scripture passages such as Matthew 5-7, Romans 12-13, I Corinthians 12-13, Galatians 5, Ephesians 4-6 that speak of our duties toward God and neighbor.

"Feelings" may make a great song, but does nothing for our interior life. Right and wrong, good and evil, are not based on "feelings." To insure that our lives are *not* governed by subjective "feelings," God not only planted the natural moral law in our very natures, He gave us the Ten Commandments and the Magisterium of the Church to interpret the law for us. It is by following these commands and heeding the guidance of the Church that we are assured peace and sanctity. The Magisterium of the Church warns us of errors and corrects us when we go astray. When we challenge, ignore or blatantly violate the teaching of the Magisterium we place our souls in jeopardy. Besides, it's a lack of love toward God. Fr. Hardon reminds us: "Christ our Lord could not have been plainer: 'Anyone who receives My commandments and keeps them will be the one who loves Me.' Notice, 'and keeps them' and again, 'if anyone loves Me he will keep My word.' He will not just hear it. He will not just tell me, 'Lord, I love you;' he will show it."[1]

In *Splendor of the Truth,* John Paul II points out: "God, who alone is good, knows perfectly what is good for man, and by virtue of His very love proposes this good to man in the commandments."[2]

He continues: "Keeping God's law in particular situations can be difficult, extremely difficult, but it is never impossible. This is the constant teaching of the Church's tradition....For God does not command the impossible, but in commanding He admonishes you to do what you can and to pray for what you cannot, and He gives His aid to enable you. His commandments are not burdensome (Jn. 5:3); His yoke is easy and His burden light (Mt. 11:30)."[3]

Columnist Fr. Robert D. Smith in an article titled "The Central Mystery" reminds us that "The central teaching of Christ and His Church is that all people on earth, non-Catholic as well as Catholic, must repent of their sins against the Ten Commandments in order to be save. The Ten Commandments are not to be understood as one thing for one group, and as another thing for another group, but as the same for all. The killing of an innocent person, abortion, gratuitous rudeness, theft...are all acts of dishonor for everyone who commits them...A non-Catholic or even, possibly, a Catholic, upon first taking up one of these activities, may not see the evil in it, may not see the intrinsic dishonor in it. But not long-term. The evil of it will penetrate. Long-term invincible ignorance, ignorance in good faith, is impossible on the basic questions of universal moral law."[4]

---

[1]Op. cit. *Spiritual Life In The Modern World,* p. 53.
[2]*The Splendor of Truth,* op. cit., n.35.
[3]Ibid, n.102.
[4]Fr. Robert D. Smith "The Central Mystery, " Jan. 4, 1996 column, p. 2.

Let's digress for a moment and consider vincible ignorance and invincible ignorance. Vincible ignorance is ignorance that could have been overcome. The person laboring under this ignorance has been guilty of negligence and is responsible for the resulting error of judgment and moral responsibility. For example, if we know that the Holy Father or the Church has spoken on a specific moral situation but through laziness refuse to learn or read about the Church's stand, we are guilty of vincible ignorance. We could learn the truth but we don't want to know it. But if our error of judgment is the result of invincible ignorance, or ignorance that cannot be overcome after reasonable diligence in trying to find out the truth, one is not guilty of the error of judgment and this excuses us from moral responsibility.

The Ten Commandments, the Precepts of the Church, and the spiritual and corporal works of mercy[5] are not just a series of dos and don'ts, but actually a blueprint for peace and happiness. God isn't trying to be a killjoy by imposing these on us. Rather, He wants us to live in joy and happiness now. Just image what a wonderful world this would be if people truly tried to live by God's law! In addition, the commandments help us to fulfill our vocation to live in Christ. Sins against the commandments not only turn us from our calling and Christ's love for us, but destroy peace in our hearts and in our world.

A priest told a story about a man in his mid-fifties going to confession and confessing that he disobeyed his mother. While amusing, the point of the story was that we can get stuck in a grade school mentality when it comes to God's law and our sins. Each commandment has such depth. For that reason each will be explained in detail. This is not to frighten us, make us despair, or cause us to be scrupulous. It's rather to educate us to the areas in which we should work so that we can deepen our love of God as we persevere in our daily struggle. As we discuss the various sins that can be committed against the Commandments, the Precepts, and the works of mercy, I will indicate when a sin is a mortal sin by either calling it a mortal sin or a grave sin. These words are interchangeable. Grave or mortal sin describes the spiritual reality of cutting ourselves off

---

[5] *Basic Catechism* (Boston: Daughters of St. Paul, 1984), pp. 20-23.

from God and His graces. Should we die in the state of mortal/grave sin, we forever exclude ourselves from Heaven.

THE TEN COMMANDMENTS

1. I, the Lord, am your God. You shall not have other gods besides me.
2. You shall not take the name of the Lord, your God, in vain.
3. Remember to keep holy the Lord's day.
4. Honor your father and your mother.
5. You shall not kill.
6. You shall not commit adultery.
7. You shall not steal.
8. You shall not bear false witness against your neighbor.
9. You shall not covet your neighbor's wife.
10. You shall not covet anything that belongs to your neighbor.

I, am the Lord your God.
You shall not have other gods besides Me

The first commandment (The *Catholic Catechism* #2084-2141) directs us to not only worship God, but to put Him first in our lives. Society elevates sex, amusement, money, comfort, and power above God and His commands. It is our obligation to redirect our lives and lead society to render to God above all love and honor. We do it through prayer, sacrifice, devotion, and adoration.

In addition, we should show love and respect to anything that refers to God and those persons who are close to God such as our Blessed Mother, the angels and the saints. Since we are social beings, we not only honor God through private prayers and devotions, but also through public worship. Yes, we can pray to God in the woods, but we still have to keep our Sunday obligation to attend Mass because this is to worship God as a community on the day of His Son's resurrection. It is also the first precept of the Church. This commandment also includes our obligations toward the virtues of faith, hope, and charity.

Sins against the first commandment include: idolatry, irreligion, superstition, tempting God, sacrilege, and simony. By their very nature they can be mortal sins.

Idolatry: While we might not worship water or fire, we may put a job, sports, hobbies, our children, or materialism before

God. These can become our gods if we are not careful. Idolatry makes divine what is not of God. Belief in goddesses, Wicca, New Age religious ceremonies, witchcraft, the occult, black magic, devil worship, ancestor or state worship, and Satanism are grave sins against God. In addition, Fr. John Hardon, SJ, writes: "Modern forms of worshipping false gods are secularism, which claims that this world is the only one worth living for; hedonism, which makes earthly pleasure its only aim; and Communism, which denies the existence of God and looks to man's happiness in a classless society in this life and not in the life to come."[6]

Irreligion: This mortal sin is the total failure to worship God. This sin runs rampant through our world today and is particularly visible on college campuses.

Superstition: The attribution of divine powers to created things is another sin against God. This includes spiritism, fortune-telling, horoscopes, astrology, psychics, tarot cards, interpretation of omens, sorcery (even to restore health), charms, palmistry, clairvoyance, mediums, and the ouija board. As Catholics, we have to be very wary of being pulled into any of the above. Dabbling in the occult is dangerous. Fr. Gabrielle Amorth, the official exorcist for the diocese of Rome revealed that there was a "great rise in occult practices in Italy and this was leading to the possession of many people, especially women."[7] Today, most of this type of activity is cleverly disguised and comes to us under the heading of "The New Age Movement."

Tempting God: This sin is demanding from God something that we have no right to expect. It's testing God. It demands extraordinary intervention for something that we can resolve by fulfilling our obligations. Examples include praying to win the lottery to pay the bills when we can cut back on our expenses, or placing ourselves in senseless danger and expecting God to protect us.

---

[6]John A. Hardon, SJ, *The Question and Answer Catholic Catechism* (Garden City, NY: Doubleday Image Book, 1981), p.128.
[7]*Inside the Vatican,* (January 1994) quoted in the book *Call of the Ages* by Thomas W. Petrisko (Santa Barbara: Queenship Publishing Co., 1995) p.145.

Sacrilege: Sacrilege is the mistreatment of that which is consecrated to God, be it a thing, a person, or a place. All that is consecrated to God's service must be treated with reverence. If we make a bad confession, receive Holy Communion or other sacraments of the living while in the state of mortal sin, we commit the additional sin of sacrilege.

Simony: This sin consists of attempting to buy or sell spiritual benefits. It is a sin against the honor due to God, for God's grace cannot be exchanged for money or used for temporal gains.

The ***Catechism of the Catholic Church*** points out that: "The first commandment requires us to nourish and protect our faith with prudence and vigilance, and to reject everything that is opposed to it."[8] Other sins against the first commandment include religious indifferentism, unbelief, atheism, apostasy, heresy, schism, deliberate doubt, and placing our faith in danger. These are all sins against faith and are grave sins by their very nature. They are a combination of widespread errors that contend that one religion is as good as another. Therefore it implies a denial of the truth of Christian revelation, or even of the existence of God. They disdain the enlightenment of God's word and refuse to bow to God's authority.

Religious indifferentism: This widespread error contends that one religion is as good as another. Therefore it implies a denial of the truth of Christian revelation. While it is sinful for Catholics to believe this error, people of other faiths may hold this view with involuntary ignorance; therefore they are not morally guilty.

Unbelief: The person who disdains the enlightenment of God's word and refuses to bow to God's authority, preferring to follow his or her own feelings and opinions, commits the sin of unbelief. *Atheism,* on the other hand, denies the existence and our dependence on God.

Apostasy is the rejection of the true religion by a former believer or the total rejection of Jesus Christ and His teachings by a former believer while h*eresy* is committed by one who refuses to give assent to one or several articles of faith without denying all the truths of Christian revelation. The writings of

---

[8]*Catechism of the Catholic Church,* op. cit., n.2088.

the Holy Father and the *Catechism of the Catholic Church* are must reading if we wish to be guided by truth.

Schism is committed by those who separate themselves from the legitimate authority of the Church. *Deliberate Doubt,* like heresy, is committed by deliberately accepting doubts against the faith. We commit this sin when we disregard or refuse to believe what God has revealed or what the Church teaches. Such a person also commits the sin of heresy. It is important to remember that many points of our faith are based on divine mysteries. We cannot understand them with our finite minds.

Deliberately placing self in near occasions of sin is a sin against faith. Reading books, pamphlets, articles, and other such materials that are against the Catholic faith and Christian morals is deliberately placing oneself in a near occasion of sin against faith. Other occasions include attending services of other religions without sufficient cause. It is not a sin to attend non-Catholic funerals, weddings, christenings or ecumenical prayer services approved by the Church. It would be a mortal sin to join an organization such as Freemasonry.

Despair and presumption, which are sins against hope, likewise are included under the first commandment. They are grave sins by their very nature. *Despair* is a deliberate refusal to hope for or appeal to God's mercy. *Presumption* is the false hope that God will save us without our effort, or the false hope that we can be saved with our effort alone and with no need of God's help. We can presume on God's mercy by "hoping to obtain His forgiveness without conversion and glory without merit."[9]

Sins against charity are also attached to the first commandment. They include indifference, ingratitude, lukewarmness, spiritual sloth, and hatred of God. "*Indifference* neglects or refuses to reflect on divine charity;...*Ingratitude* fails or refuses to acknowledge divine charity and to return Him love for love. *Lukewarmness* is hesitation or negligence in responding to divine love;..."[10] Spiritual *sloth* was discussed in the last chapter. *Hatred of God* is the greatest sin and the greatest disorder. It

---

[9]Ibid, n.2092.
[10]Ibid, n.2094.

comes from pride. Those guilty of this sin curse God because He inflicts punishments and forbids sins.

Under the first commandment we also consider the fulfillment of the promises and vows we made to God when we received the sacraments of Baptism, Confirmation, Matrimony or Holy Orders. If we have joined a religious order, third order, or taken private vows, are we faithful to our commitment?

You Shall Not Take The Name Of The Lord, Your God, In Vain

The first commandment also includes the second and third commandments. It is our duty to honor God and that honor extends to His name (God) along with the name of Jesus, the second person of the Blessed Trinity. This commandment (The *Catholic Catechism* #2142-2167) also forbids the improper use of the names of Our Lady, the angels, the saints, and the Holy Church with her sacraments. It is sinful for us to casually use these sacred names in anger, casual conversation, or oaths. Sins against this commandment include false promises, blasphemy, cursing, profanity, perjury, false and illicit oaths, and vows.

We misuse God's name when we make a *false promise* to someone in His name and then renege. By doing this, we make God out to be a liar.

Blasphemy is the thought, action, or the use of insulting speech to express contempt for God, His saints and holy things. This a mortal sin when full intention and consent are given. We see this sometimes in art, books, and movies. *Cursing* "is calling down evil on someone or something."[11] *Profanity* is taking the Lord's name in vain, either out of rage, surprise, or other emotions. It can be a grave sin if there is deliberate disrespect and full awareness. Normally it is a venial sin.

Perjury is using the name of God to swear to a false promise, or it calls on God to witness a lie. This is violating the holiness of God's name. This is a grave sin. In regard to *oaths*, if truthfulness and justice are missing, taking an oath would be mortally sinful. If one should fail to fulfill a valid promise (made under oath), he would commit a sin. Its gravity would

---

[11]*The Question and Answer Catholic Catechism*, op. cit., p.130.

depend on the importance of the thing promised. Similarly, the breaking of a *vow* is a sin; its gravity depends on the importance of the matter and on the intention of binding oneself to that particular action.

Under this commandment, parents, pastors, and sponsors are to ensure that children receive a name that is not in opposition to Catholic beliefs. That is why we have the custom of naming our children after saints, Our Lady, a virtue (e.g. Prudence) or mystery such as the Incarnation.

Remember To Keep Holy The Lord's Day

While the above is what we normally consider the third commandment (The *Catholic Catechism* #2168-2195), the Old Testament includes the addition "...thou shall not work on this day."[12] This commandment establishes a specific day for us to worship God and to rest from our work for the sake of our souls. The Church established Sunday as the day to worship God through the sacrifice of the Holy Mass because this was the day of the resurrection of Our Lord. Those who are at least seven years old and who have attained sufficient reason are obliged to attend Mass Saturday evening or on Sunday. To miss Holy Mass is to commit a mortal sin. We are excused from this obligation if we are ill, need to care for others who cannot be left alone, the distance to attend Mass is too great, or if there are other difficult circumstances that we have discussed with a confessor. Besides being physically present at Mass, we have to be attentive and participate. It's a venial sin to come late or to leave early. To hear Mass, we must be there for the three principal parts of the Liturgy of the Eucharist; that is, the Offertory, the Consecration, and the priest's Communion. If we miss one of these through our own fault, we have not fulfilled our Sunday obligation.

We are also obliged to rest rather than work on Sunday. This time of rest gives us the opportunity to worship God and perform the works of mercy. It also provides a change of pace that fosters peace, enjoyment, and relaxation. It is a day when we can visit family, friends, the sick, the elderly and the housebound. The Sabbath rest also provides us with a chance to

---

[12]Ex. 20: 8-10.

read, reflect, meditate and do cultural activities. Sunday rest is intended to allow the mind to dwell on divine things (prayer), to rejoice in God's gifts to us (i.e., family), to give the soul the needed distraction from merely temporal things and material concerns (recreation). Employers have an obligation toward employees to see that they have an opportunity to worship God along with time for rest. As Christians, we should be careful not to make undo demands on others on Sunday so that they can observe the Lord's day. For example, by shopping on Sunday, we encourage stores to remain open thereby making it difficult for clerks to get to church or have a day of rest. As citizens, we should work to have Sundays and the holy days recognized as legal holidays.[13]

Since not all labor can be avoided, there are exceptions that are permitted: when this labor is necessary for oneself or for others, as in the case of necessary household work, care of the sick, or other kinds of services that the common good requires.

Honor Your Father And Your Mother

The fourth commandment directs us to honor, respect, help, and obey our parents (while we are subject to them) (The *Catholic Catechism* 2197-2257). "Children sin against the respect they owe their parents by speaking unkindly to or about them, by striking or insulting them, and being ashamed of them."[14] Additional sins against parents include *unkindness, disrespect,* and *neglect of their needs. Disobedience* is the main sin of children of minor age. As children mature and leave home, they are still bound to listen to the advice and anticipate the wishes of their parents, and accept corrections. The book of Proverbs teaches: *"A wise son hears his father's instruction, but a scoffer does not listen to rebuke."*[15] As parents age, it is the obligation of children to give moral, physical and financial support when needed. We should be with them when they are ill, lonely or upset. The book of Sirach reminds us: *"Whoever honors his father atones for sins, and whoever glorifies his mother*

---

[13]*The Catechism of the Catholic Church,* #2188.
[14]Ibid, p.137.
[15]Prov. 13:1.

*is like one who lays up treasure. Whoever honors his father will
be gladdened by his own children, and when he prays he will be
heard. Whoever glorifies his father will have long life, and whoever obeys the Lord will refresh his mother.*"[16]

We are also obliged to show affection and gratitude toward
our parents and ancestors. They gave us life. In addition, this
commandment promotes harmony rather than rivalry among
brothers and sisters. Respect and gratitude are also owed to
those from whom we received the gift of faith and the sacraments. This may include grandparents, other family members,
pastors, teachers, godparents or friends.

Parents, on the other hand, have the serious obligation to
care for the material *and spiritual needs of their children.* Not
only are we obliged to feed, care, and house our children, we
must also provide for their spiritual and secular education. As
parents, we are obligated to educate our children not only in the
faith but also in the virtues through word and example.

The family, as the domestic church, is called to evangelize
its members. Family prayer and reading Scripture together not
only strengthens family bonds but also increases the practice of
charity within the family. It is the responsibility of the family,
not the government, to care for the young, the elderly, the sick,
the handicapped, and the poor. In situations where this is not
possible, the principle of subsidiary should be applied. This is
when social agencies step in to help.

The fourth commandment also includes honoring and obey-
ing those in authority in the Church, in civil government, in our
place of employment, school, and other institutions. Since all
authority comes from God, parents, the Church and civil au-
thorities, politicians, teachers, and other legitimate superiors are
accountable to God for their actions. We are not to obey any law
that is contrary to the law of God. Judge Joseph W. Moylan is a
courageous example in this regard. A juvenile court judge for
over 20 years in Omaha, Nebraska, he resigned his position after refusing to approve a teenager's request to waive the require-
ment that she seek her parents' approval for an abortion. In re-

---

[16]Sir. 3:2-6.

signing he noted: "I simply cannot enter an order authorizing one human life to put to death another totally innocent human being...I am reminded of Lincoln's statement: 'No law can give me the right to do what is wrong.'"[17]

The state has the obligation to insure that couples have the freedom to marry, and to establish a family without government interference or harassment. The state also is obliged to protect the moral and religious convictions of families along with the institution of marriage.

Duties of citizens include paying just taxes, being informed voters, and defending one's country.

You Shall Not Kill

The fifth commandment protects life—from conception to natural death (The *Catholic Catechism* #2258-2317). While this commandment protects both the physical and the supernatural life of man, it does not include plant or animal life since these are at the service and welfare of humanity. It would be wrong, however, to torture or kill an animal out of anger or cruelty.

The evils that fall under this commandment include: murder (which includes infanticide, parricide, fratricide), abortion, feticide, sterilization, vasectomy, euthanasia (mercy killing), suicide, genocide, rioting, hatred, gluttony, drunkenness, the use, production or sale of drugs, kidnapping, hostage taking, terrorism, physical or mental torture, slavery, prostitution and the trafficking in women and children, physical and verbal violence. These are mortal sins. Other grave sins are exposing someone to danger without grave reason and refusing to help someone in danger. Employers who pay unjust wages or physically abuse employees with degrading working conditions or unreasonable length of working hours may be guilty of indirect homicide. When countries are suffering from famines, we are obliged to come to their aid with food.

Depending on the harm done to another, the following sins can either be mortal or venial: bad example, wishing evil to oth-

---

[17]Omaha World Herald, 10/8/94.

ers, scandal, discord, disruption of peace, fights, quarrels, angry words, antagonism, refusal to interact with someone, the "silent treatment," tantrums, selfishness, pride, vanity, presumption, the desire to dominate others and the disorder of sense pleasures. Scandal is leading another into sin either through words or actions. Scandal is not only committed by individuals, it can be provoked by opinion, fashion, institutions, laws or the media.

Likewise it is sinful to incite someone to anger by selfish actions or words, snide comments, pettiness, insults, cutting remarks, bossiness, or by being inconsiderate.

In regard to our health, we are to avoid the abuse of drugs, tobacco, alcohol and food. It is a grave sin to endanger another's life through drunk-driving or excessive speed. Research or experimentation is gravely wrong if it exposes an individual to avoidable risks or when the subject does not give an informed consent. Organ transplants are morally wrong if the donor does not give his consent. In addition, it is morally wrong to take an organ that will mutilate, disable or kill one person to prolong the life of another. An example of this is found in China where prisoners are killed to harvest organs for the Western world in return for needed capital.

The fifth commandment does not forbid capital punishment, self-defense or just wars (The *Catholic Catechism* #2266). In the *Gospel of Life*, John Paul II qualifies this by saying, "the nature and the extent of the punishment must be carefully evaluated and decided upon, and ought not go to the extreme of executing the offender except in cases of absolute necessity: in other words, when it would not be possible otherwise to defend society."[18]

You Shall Not Commit Adultery

The sixth and ninth commandments complement each other and direct us to practice purity of action along with purity of thought and desire. The sixth commandment promotes the practice of chastity which is purity in conduct and intention (The

---

[18]John Paul II, *The Gospel of Life* (Boston: St. Paul Books & Media, 1995), #56.

Catholic Catechism #2331-2400). Chastity protects marriages and families, develops the individual, and nourishes peace and harmony in society. Since we are temples of the Holy Spirit, we should cultivate a deep respect for human sexuality along with moderation of the sexual instinct.

Sins against chastity are any deliberate thought, word, desire, or action by which the sexual appetite is aroused outside of marriage, and even within marriage when contrary to its purpose. These would include: adultery, fornication (sexual relations outside of marriage), all forms of artificial contraception ("the Pill," IUD, Norplant, diaphragms, foams, condoms, withdrawal), incest, homosexual acts, pornography, passionate or French kissing, petting or necking (outside of marriage). We can also commit sins against the sixth commandment by reading immoral books, or seeing immoral plays, movies, videos, or TV shows, or engaging in impure conversation or jokes. Even viewing the graphic video jackets in video stores can be a source of temptation or sin.

You Shall Not Steal

The seventh and tenth commandments complement each other and direct us to practice justice in our actions as well as in our thoughts and desires. The seventh commandment forbids keeping what belongs to another along with the unjust damage or destruction of someone else's property (The *Catholic Catechism* #2401-2463). It commands us to respect and care for the property and possessions of others, and to return them promptly when borrowed. It also commands us to honor our agreements and to pay our just debts promptly so as not to cause hardship to others. Sins against this commandment also include: theft, petty theft, robbery, business fraud, corruption, usury (excessive interest rates), unjust gains, discrimination, using people as mere objects of profit, slavery, abuse of material creation, the acceptance of bribes, unfair taxation, tax evasion, forgery of checks and invoices, excessive expenses and waste, violating contracts or promises, copying audio or video cassettes without permission, shoplifting, compulsive gambling or shopping, vandalism, employee theft, cheating on tests, cheating an employer, customer, etc., shoddy workmanship, defective merchandise, price fixing, unjust wages and misappropriation of funds. The gravity of the sin depends on the amount of money involved and the hardship incurred by the victim. For sins against the seventh commandment to be forgiven, restitution must be made or at least attempted.

Civil and public officials dealing with tax moneys must use the money wisely for the common good not personal or political gain. Unions may morally strike when it is unavoidable, not when the objectives are not for the common good nor directly linked to working conditions. Violence associated with strikes is morally unacceptable. Management and labor should cooperate through sincere negotiations to avoid the conflicts arising from strikes and lockouts.

If we are in management positions, owners of companies, or providers of services, we should consider if we are charging a fair price for our goods or services or are we price gouging? As employers, do we pay just wages so that our employees can live with dignity? Those in the medical and legal professions should consider the rates they charge. Many families are financially ruined by large medical or legal fees.

Perhaps there is a need to stop and do a little mental reflecting on the list of evils we have covered so far. Pretty long list, huh? Why all of these sins are listed is the important consideration. It is not an implication that we are guilty of most of these offenses in our lives. It is simply an attempt to show to what extremes Satan has gone to in attempting to lure our souls away from our Creator in favor of his lies and deceit. Indeed, he has produced a veritable and endless laundry list of evils.

The other reason for detailing so many potential offenses in our lives is to make it easier for us to prepare for the Sacrament of Reconciliation. It gives us a more complete and overall view of just where we are at in our own lives in relation to God's guidelines. And, of course, the Ten Commandments provide us with the best evaluation. Now back to the rest of the Commandments.

You Shall Not Bear False Witness Against Your Neighbor

Greater than wealth is our good name and reputation. As St. Paul tells us, the truth should always be on our lips. Besides being truthful in our speech and in relations with others, we should also avoid false statements or innuendoes. The eighth commandment forbids: lies, libel, perjury, rash judgment, detraction, slander, and calumny (The **Catholic Catechism** #2464-2513). A *lie* is an untrue, half-true, or inaccurate statement. *Libel* is the verbal or written attack or defamation of another so that he or she will be held in contempt. *Perjury* is a "violation of an oath or vow either by swearing to what is untrue or by omission to do what has been promised under oath."[19] *Rash Judgment* assumes the moral faults of another, while d*etraction* is the sin whereby we make known the hidden faults of another without sufficient reason. This is also known as *gossip*. The sins of *calumny* or *slander* are committed when faults or sins are falsely attributed to another. These are all sins against truthfulness and justice. Libel, perjury, detraction, calumny, and slander are grave sins. Lies, gossip, and rash judgment can either be venial or mortal sins depending on the damage done and the intention in doing the damage.

Flattery (adulation) is a sin against truthfulness going in the other direction...because it consists of speaking falsely about the qualities of another to gain something from him. *Disclosing a secret* we have been asked to keep is a sin against justice and this commandment as would be the *breaking of promises* or *contracts* and *loquacity*.

Loquacity is the bad habit of speaking excessively and without reflection. This lack of moderation in talking can lead to *exaggeration, lies, revelation of secrets and confidential knowledge, detraction, and slander*. Great harm can be done by this lack of self-control. The gravity of sins against this commandment depends on the extent of harm done. A person is obliged to make up for the harm that he or she causes by misusing speech or the written word. This applies not only to individuals, but also to the public media.

You Shall Not Covet Your Neighbor's Wife

We are composed of spirit and body. Original sin causes us to experience a certain tension between the two. As noted before, the sixth and the ninth commandment complement each other and direct us to practice temperance, generosity, purity

---

[19]*Webster's New Collegiate Dictionary.*

and chastity (The ***Catholic Catechism*** #2514-2533). We are told that only the pure of heart will see God in eternity, while purity here below provides the means to view the world through the eyes of God. Purity of heart requires prayer, self-control, decency, patience, modesty and discretion.

While the sixth commandment refers to external acts against chastity, the ninth refers to thoughts and desires. Any deliberate consent to *impure thoughts or desires* are sins against this commandment. By wearing *immodest or seductive clothing* or by engaging in *lewd conduct* we not only sin, but we can cause others to sin against this commandment. *Divorce and re-marriage* without a Church annulment are also against this commandment. These sins are mortal if there is full knowledge and consent.

You Shall Not Covet Anything That Belongs To Your Neighbor

The final commandment asks us to be detached from earthly materialism (The ***Catholic Catechism*** #2534-2557). Christ reminds us, *"Where your treasure is, there will your heart be also."*[20] Avarice, the capital sin we discussed earlier, draws us to covet what is not ours but may belong to or is owed to another. By practicing custody of the eyes, self-control in regard to "wants," humility, detachment, and abandonment to God, avarice can be controlled.

The tenth commandment forbids *greed* or *covetousness by thoughts and desires of another's property or possessions.* This sin can also lead to *envy* and *jealousy* that can be either mortal or venial depending on the intention, gravity, and circumstances. On the positive side, it commands generosity in the use of our material goods for God and those in need.

PRECEPTS OF THE CHURCH

Besides keeping the Ten Commandments, we are also obligated to keep the laws of the Church. They are:

1. "You shall attend Mass on Sundays and holy days of obligation.*"[21]

---

[20]Mt. 6:21.
[21]Cf. CIC, cann. 1246-1248; CCEO, can. 881.

*Christmas, December 25

Solemnity of the Mother of God, January 1

Ascension Thursday (40th day after Easter)

The Assumption, August 15

All Saints Day, November 1

The Immaculate Conception, December 8

2. "You shall confess your grave sins at least once a year."[22]

3. "You shall humbly receive your Creator in Holy Communion at least during the Easter season."[23]

4. "You shall keep holy the holy days of obligation."[24]

5. "You shall observe the prescribed days of fasting and abstinence."[25]

6. "You shall observe the laws of the Church regarding marriage."[26]

7. The faithful also have the duty of providing for the material needs of the Church, each according to his abilities.[27]

These Precepts of the Church were established to help us fulfill the first Commandment. To violate these precepts is a mortal sin. The faithful also have the duty to join in the missionary spirit and apostolate of the Church. We do this through our alms and the example of upright moral lives.

In addition we are obliged to practice the spiritual and corporal works of mercy, the latter of which are based on the Gospel passage found in St. Matthew 25:31-46. Through daily living opportunities arise to perform the works of mercy in a variety of ways. When these occasions arise, how do we respond? If we had the chance to perform one of the works and we did not because of laziness, human respect, selfishness, or a lack of generosity, we committed a sin. The gravity of the sin is dependent on the seriousness of the circumstances and our intention. As St. Rose of Lima told her mother, "When we serve the poor and the sick, we serve Jesus. We must not fail to help our neighbors, because in them we serve Jesus."[28]

---

[22]Cf. CIC, cann. 989, CCEO, can 719.

[23]Cf. CIC, cann 920; CCEO, can. 708; 881.

[24]Cf. CIC, cann. 1246; CCEO, can. 881.

[25]Cf. CIC, cann. 1249-1251; CCEO, can. 882.

[26]Cf, CIC, cann. 1108.

[27]Cf CIC cann. 222.

[28]P. Hansen, *Vita Mirabilis* (Louvain, 1668).

THE WORKS OF MERCY

Spiritual

1. To admonish the sinner.
2. To instruct the ignorant.
3. To counsel the doubtful.
4. To comfort the sorrowful.
5. To bear wrongs patiently.
6. To forgive all injuries.
7. To pray for the living and the dead.

Corporal

1. To feed the hungry.
2. To give drink to the thirsty.
3. To clothe the naked.
4. To visit the imprisoned.
5. To shelter the homeless.
6. To visit the sick.
7. To bury the dead.

To Admonish The Sinner

The "live and let live attitude" has opened our culture to the acceptance of every perversion possible. Parents should not simply accept the "living together" of their sons or daughters, the homosexual lifestyle, or divorce and remarriage. This is not admonishing the sinner. While we love our children, family members, and friends, we cannot justify, condone, accept, or glorify their sins. For example, it is scandalous of us to involve family and friends in showers and parties for "couples living together." It has also become common for parents to give contraceptives to their single daughters or to provide alcohol for underage parties that results in drunkenness. These actions are not only wrong, they are mortal sins. To do nothing when objectionable "sex education" is taught in grade and high schools is gravely wrong.

We have countless opportunities through our example and conversation to help others live in a manner pleasing to God. When people discuss abortion, euthanasia, or other moral problems, we can courageously interject the Christian point of view. If people begin to gossip, we can tactfully change the subject. We can also encourage friends and family members to attend retreats, missions, and days of recollection. When we do, we play an important role in the rechristianization of the world. We are our "brother's keeper."

To Instruct The Ignorant

As parents, we have the primary responsibility to hand down the truths of faith and the pious practices through our word and example. Do we pray as a family? A family rosary?

Do we set a time to read Bible stories and the lives of the saints to our children? Do we teach them doctrine at home?

Unfortunately, many adults are ignorant of their faith. We can help friends and relatives to know Our Lord better by inviting them to attend doctrinal study classes with us or passing on concise and easy to understand books on doctrine and morality. We can show them doctrinally sound videos or lend them audio tapes. Spiritual reading is important, as is devoting some time to sound religious teaching on cable TV networks such as EWTN. Introduce friends to Mother Angelica's TV station, to increase their knowledge of scripture, doctrine, and morality. Mother also has a short-wave radio station for those who prefer to listen rather than watch or who do not have access to EWTN on cable TV.

The pro-life movement is another aspect of this work. As we have seen in the fifth commandment we have an obligation to protect the unborn. In addition, we have to clearly explain to pro-abortionists why abortion is morally evil. We should pray for the virtue of fortitude and then speak to our friends whose lives are contrary to the teachings of the Church. It has been said that the only way evil can triumph is for good people to do nothing. We can also practice this work of mercy by writing letters to editors of magazines and newspapers (as well as managers of radio and television stations) to complain about objectionable material appearing in their media.

To Counsel The Doubtful

Often our children, relatives, and friends come to us with doubts about their faith or relationship with God. If we listen, we can help them to seek and find the truth. If we do not know the answer, we are obliged to ask a priest or research the question in moral theology books or the **Catechism of the Catholic Church**. Take the person to confession where he or she can discuss the matter with a priest in more detail. We will receive the grace to counsel the doubtful if we deepen our own prayer life by meditating on sacred Scripture and reading other spiritual books; pray for the gifts of the Holy Spirit; strive to grow in virtue; try to attend daily Mass and frequent confession.

To Comfort the Sorrowful

In times of sorrow many people feel abandoned. Sometimes we do not know what to say or do for persons who are suffering, so we separate ourselves from them. As Christians we must make an effort to help those who are going through hard times. Perhaps all we have to do is listen. At other times we can give practical help such as bringing a hot meal, offering to baby-sit, or providing transportation and financial help.

It is also important to reassure the suffering that what they are experiencing is not a punishment from God but actually a way that God uses to bring them closer to Him.

Bear Wrongs Patiently

No one can escape the injustices of life. As spouses we sometimes hurt each other. We can be mistreated by friends, betrayed by our business associates, ignored by our children, slandered by our acquaintances, or wounded by relatives. By bearing these wrongs patiently we unite ourselves more intimately with Christ. If accepted in the spirit of patience, these injustices can lead us to great spiritual heights. When we lash out at those who wrong us we stunt our spiritual growth. We can offer these personal hurts to Our Lord in reparation for all the injustices in the world.

Forgive All Injuries

It's difficult at times to forgive those who hurt us. When we refuse to be reconciled with those who wound us, we hurt ourselves spiritually, emotionally, and sometimes physically. If we hold grudges, Christ tells us that we have to leave our gift at the altar and be reconciled before we can even pray.[29] Grudges hinder our spiritual growth and if prolonged can kill our souls through bitterness. The vice of pride is usually the culprit in our reluctance to forgive. By imitating the humility of Christ, we can stifle our pride and learn to forgive. Only then will we have peace in our hearts, in our homes, and in the world.

Pray For The Living And The Dead

This work of mercy has a twofold purpose. We are counseled to offer prayers for those passing through life and for those who have passed on to another life. During Mass, through our rosary intentions, in our personal mental prayer, we can pray for our families, friends, business associates, for those who

---

[29]Matt. 5:23.

ask for our prayers, and for the souls of our loved ones in purgatory. We can also extend our prayers to those most in need of God's mercy, whether living or dead.

Another way that we can pray for the living and the dead is by offering our work for them. By saying the Morning Offering when we begin the day, we turn our whole day—every action, thought, word, and deed—into prayer. We can offer household chores for our children, lawn chores for our spouses, and paperwork for our business associates. Irksome tasks no longer seem to bother us when we offer them for the conversion of the world and sinners.

Feed The Hungry

The traditional approach for this first corporal work of mercy is to donate food, time, or money to food pantries, soup kitchens, and meals on wheels. Meals delivered to those sick or new mothers are a great work of charity. At Thanksgiving and Christmastime the holiday spirit moves us to donate food baskets to the needy and money to the missions. Another way that we can help the hungry is to donate money, time, and talent to Catholic Charities, Catholic Relief, Share, and other agencies trying to help the plight of those struggling financially. A lesser-known way of fulfilling this work of mercy is to entertain those who cannot reciprocate.

If we lower our expectations and standards of wants, we can give more to those who have less. By developing a simpler lifestyle ourselves, we can help others, not only at holiday time but throughout the year.

Give Drink To The Thirsty

Families with children fulfill this work of mercy twenty-four hours a day. This seemingly insignificant act actually develops a spirit of service in our lives. Through it we become more sensitive to the people around us. We develop the ability to anticipate needs such as a thirsty mail carrier, repairman, painter, or the child mowing our lawns. Offering a cup of coffee to a friend who stops by or inviting a neighbor over for a glass of lemonade stems from the virtue of charity and is a work of mercy. It leads us to become more patient with those who become ill or need our help. Anyone who has sat at the bedside of an ailing or dying person knows that much of the time is spent moistening the patient's lips and giving them sips of water.

Clothe The Naked

In addition to the Thanksgiving clothing drive, we can donate clean clothing year-round to charitable organizations. Outgrown clothing can be passed down to friends, neighbors, relatives, and Catholic Charities. Pro-life groups can always use baby clothes and furniture. So many things that can be reused by those in need are tossed out through laziness. When shopping, rather than buying two items for ourselves, why not buy one and purchase the other for an elderly person on a fixed income? By developing a simpler lifestyle we can donate our excess financial resources to relieve the problems of those less fortunate. The greater our material blessings, the greater our obligation is toward others.

Visit The Imprisoned

We can fulfill this work of mercy in person, through letters, donations to prison apostolates, and prayers. Letters alleviate loneliness, despair, and possibly the loss of faith. Prison chaplains are always in need of Catholic books, videos, magazines, rosaries, and medals.

Those who live in nursing homes or who are confined to mental institutions may very well be considered "imprisoned." So too are those confined to their homes while caring for small children, an elderly parent, or a loved one in need of constant attention. We can stop by to see these people, drop off a cake to brighten their day, or bring a picnic lunch to share with them. Maybe we can baby-sit for the young mother, provide transportation, or relieve a family member for a day. When we cannot get out, we can telephone.

Shelter The Homeless

For parents, this work of mercy begins when they bring their first baby home from the hospital. It also includes the responsibility of reaching out to relatives and friends who need a place to stay. Those who adopt children or become foster parents are sheltering the homeless. Elderly parents who can no longer care for themselves, an adult child whose marriage has dissolved, or a relative immigrating to our country may need to find shelter with us. Another way to fulfill this work of mercy is to donate time or money to half-way houses and shelters.

Visit The Sick

We can lighten the sufferings of the sick by visits, phone calls, cards, toys, flowers, and simply caring. Each time we visit someone who is in a hospital or nursing home or a shut-in, we visit Christ. To those we visit, we *are* Christ, bringing hope and laughter to ease their sufferings. The sick and dying need our encouragement and listening ear. We can arrange for the patient to receive the anointing of the sick and the last rites. In addition, Catholic hospitals deserve our financial support and volunteer hours. Only in eternity will we know how many people entered heaven because a volunteer, nurse, priest, or visitor was there to pray with them when they were in spiritual need.

Bury The Dead

Wakes and funerals are one of the important ways we fulfill this final corporal work of mercy. We pray for the soul of the deceased while comforting the family members left behind. When the funeral is over, our obligation does not end. The survivors still need someone to talk with and possibly help in filling out forms, advice in financial matters, or physical help in disposing of possessions.

The Duties of Our State In Life

In addition, we have to consider the duties of our state of life. These duties differ for the married, the single, the religious, and priestly vocations. There are specific duties for employers and employees, management and union. If we do not fulfill these duties properly, it is matter for confession.

Besides falling into sin ourselves, we may not realize that we can also be an accessory to someone else's sin. Fr. F. X. Lasance notes this occurs by 1) counsel ("Use the pill."); 2) command ("You must have an abortion!"); 3) consent ("It's fine to cheat on your income taxes."); 4) provocation (Inciting someone to anger.); 5) praise or flattery ("You look sexy in that swimsuit."); 6) concealment; ("I'll conceal your theft."); 7) partaking ("Let's both get drunk."); 8) silence ("I know you cheated on that test but I won't tell."); 9) defense of the ill done ("The girl was desperate. She had to have the abortion.")

For those of us who find it hard to know what to say in confession, this chapter gives much material for consideration! For those who may find this chapter a bit intimidating, consider the words of Jesus to Blessed Faustina: "Souls that make an appeal to My mercy delight Me. To such souls I grant even more than they ask. I cannot punish even the greatest sinner if he makes an appeal to My Compassion...No soul that has called upon My mercy has every been disappointed...On the cross, the fountain of My mercy was opened wide by the lance for all souls—no one have I excluded!...I am Love and Mercy itself...Let no soul fear to draw near to Me, even though its sins be as scarlet...My mercy is greater than your sins and those of the entire world...I let my Sacred Heart be pierced with a lance, thus opening wide the source of mercy for you. Come then with trust to draw graces from this fountain. I never reject a contrite heart...Sooner would heaven and earth turn into nothingness than would My mercy not embrace a trusting soul."[30]

---

[30]*Divine Mercy In My Soul,* op. cit., #1146, 1541, 1182, 1074, 699, 1485, 1777.

The Importance Of Frequent Confession And Forming Our Consciences

"I'm a good Catholic.
I don't commit mortal sins.
Why should I go to confession frequently?"

When I was introduced to the benefits of weekly confession, my older daughters were five and six years old. Since the eldest was very precocious, we spent our days in a perpetual battle of the wills. After consulting with the priest, and preparation, Katie made her first confession when she was six years old. After seeing the wonderful effects of confession on our relationship, this custom of age 6 for first confession became a family tradition. Rather than being a traumatic event for our daughters, they *loved* going to confession and talking things over with "Father." One day their zeal became quite embarrassing. As I left the confessional, I found Katie and Marianne in hand-to-hand combat, wrestling on the ground in front of the confessional. The fight was over who was going to go in next!

Weekly confession caused such a radical change in our family life that my husband could tell which day we went the moment he walked in from work. His first comment would be, "You went to confession today, didn't you?" Frankly, I did find that a bit irritating but the changes in personalities, cooperation, peace, and kindness *were* noticeable. We could actually *see* the effects of sacramental and sanctifying grace; this is because the Sacrament of Penance not only forgives sins, it also gives us a specific grace to overcome the faults we confess. We even began discussing the "confession curve." The curve was at its peak the moment we left the church. As the days passed, the curve rapidly swung downward until it was time again for weekly confession. While I was tempted to skip a week for myself, I did not want to lose the family benefits by letting the girls skip a week! This custom of frequent confession is still practiced by our daughters who are now adults. It simply became part of their routine.

When a person develops the habit of going to confession weekly as a child, it is natural to continue to receive the sacrament during the turbulent teen years and the "free at last" college years. Weekly confession is the greatest safeguard of our children's chastity. It also protects our youth against drug use and drunkenness. Besides this, weekly confession helps parents and teens accept each other and work together more smoothly, thereby guaranteeing family harmony. Family controversies or problems can be resolved in the confessional. Several years ago, friends were having conflicts with their eldest daughter, who was in college. The young woman agreed to go to confession and discuss the situation with the priest. As she began her confession, there was a terrifying crash of thunder that shook the church. That was the moment of her conversion! The scare, combined with the priest's advice, restored peace in her family.

If *we* do not teach our children right and wrong, the Ten Commandments, moral principles, and virtues (good habits), they could be in serious spiritual danger by the time they are in junior high. In addition, we not only have to school them as to the primary purpose of life (to know, to love, and to serve God), but also in the reality of Heaven and Hell. As the primary educators of our children, it is our responsibility, not the Catholic school's, to instill these religious and moral principles. The school can only build on what the child is taught in the home. If this education is combined with frequent reception of the sacraments, especially the Sacrament of Reconciliation, our children will be protected from the promiscuous atmosphere around them. If we do not take this responsibility seriously, our children may fall victim to drug addiction, habitual drunkenness, fornication (premarital sex), and possibly suicide. Today these sorrows are happening in "nice" families.

For adults, frequent confession is equally important. The more we struggle to grow in virtue and root out our vices (bad habits), the more refined and sensitive our conscience becomes. Those who stay away from the Sacrament of Reconciliation easily accept the immorality presented in movies, on TV, in songs, in books or magazines, in ads, and even the example of friends, acquaintances, and family members. One's attitude becomes, "Everyone is doing it. It must be right." Today's society praises, promotes, and practices acts and activities that are morally evil. To illustrate how pervasive evil is, I purchased a small booklet in the grocery store on women's health concerns. I was stunned to see a list of mortal sins promoted as "wonderful options for a satisfying life." To save our souls today and to acquire peace of mind, we all need frequent confession. It is not an option. It is a necessity.

Natural Law And The Voice Of Conscience

St. Thomas teaches that conscience is a judgment of our practical reason about a specific good to be done, or evil to be avoided. It does not create the moral law, but applies it to a specific case. The *Catechism of the Catholic Church* explains: "Deep within his conscience man discovers a law which he has not laid upon himself but which he must obey....a law inscribed by God."[1]

This law is called the natural law. Natural law is the same for all religions, nationalities, and races. Moses told his people: *"If only you heed the voice of the Lord, your God, and keep His commandments and statues that are written in this book of the law...For this command which I enjoin on you today is not too mysterious and remote for you....No, it is something very near to you, already in your mouths and in your hearts; you have only to carry it out."*[2]

The universality of the natural law came alive for me at the UN Conference on Population and Development in Cairo, Egypt. One of the main issues at this Conference was the imposition of world-wide abortion as a means of "family planning." While the Holy See was criticized in the secular press for de-

[1]*Catechism of the Catholic Church*, op. cit., p.438.
[2]Deuteronomy 30:10-11, 14.

railing this Conference, it was actually a coalition of Latin American, African, and Moslem countries united *with* the Holy See. This diverse group united in opposition to abortion, not on religious grounds, but because it is a human concern written in the hearts of all through the natural law. An Egyptian clerk told me, "No people on our street want this, only our government. What is happening there (at the Conference) is very bad. It will destroy our marriages and our families. We are so worried."

In Egypt, I also saw the influence of natural law throughout the centuries. In the Valley of the Kings, outside of Luxor, there is the tomb of Amonhotep. In this tomb is the carefully preserved six month old *fetus* of the Pharaoh's wife. Legend has it, that the sudden death of their 9-year-old son brought on the Queen's miscarriage. In 1150 BC this royal family so cherished their preborn child that they carried out all the rites of death for this child as they did for their other son.

At the UN Conference, the influence of natural law did not end with abortion. Sterilization and contraception were also opposed by people from various religions, cultures, and countries. Faxing daily news reports from the hotel's business office, I became acquainted with the young Muslim women working there. One of the young women was engaged to be married, while the others were young married women. The engaged woman was describing the financial difficulties pregnancy would cause, so although she was "not in favor of contraception," she would use it for awhile after she was married. The other young women immediately interrupted her, explained the dangers contraception posed to her marriage, then offered to teach her natural family planning (NFP). By the time the conversation was over, the engaged woman agreed to use NFP rather than contraceptives.

In the encyclical, *The Splendor of Truth,* John Paul II explains: "...[W]hereas the natural law discloses the objective and universal demands of the moral good, conscience is the application of the law in a particular case; this application of the law thus becomes an inner dictate for the individual, a summons to do what is good in this particular situation. Conscience thus formulates *moral obligation* in the light of the natural law: it is the obligation to do what the individual, through the workings of his conscience, *knows* to be a good he is called to do here and now. The universality of the law and its obligation are acknowledged, not suppressed, once reason has established the law's application in concrete present circumstances."[3]

While our conscience commands us to do what we know is best and not to do what we know is wrong, we must be careful because "what we think" or "what we feel" is often taken as license to do whatever we want to do. Because of original sin and our fallen nature, conscience can easily be deformed and our "thinking" or "feeling" can be open to all kinds of errors and rationalizations. At other times, the ability to think is perverted by the fear of knowing the truth. The truth might be inconvenient, distasteful, or materially costly. So "doing what you think is best" becomes a license for not thinking at all.

While the truth is written in our hearts, we have the "freedom" to ignore it, bury it, or kill it. Should we do so, we create a false conscience. Out of fear of losing a professional position, a large income, wealth, material possessions, or social position, people create a false conscience. If only we realized that *God will care for us* in all our needs, fear would be eliminated. Instead, the fearful choose to remain *voluntarily ignorant* about the morality of their own actions. The price of this voluntary ignorance is one's gradual bondage to mere animal instincts. We see this in the upheaval in society. Bribes, payoffs, lies, acts of dishonesty, are all part of doing business, or so some executives, bankers, stock analysts and politicians think. Obstetricians and Gynecologists, caught in the health-care money crunch, fear losing patients (and income) if they refuse to prescribe contraceptives even if they are abortifacients. They soothe their consciences by contributing to pro-life causes. Yet the spiritual conflict remains, although buried. Archbishop Sheen explains: "It is an interesting psychological fact that the frustrated soul hates goodness and wants to be separated from it. Every sinner hides from God."[4] But we can only hide so long. Eventually the spiritual conflict erupts causing mental, physical, and even marital problems.

---

[3]John Paul II, Encyclical Letter *The Splendor of Truth*, n.59.
[4]*Peace of Soul*, op. cit., p.9

We can also have a false conscience as a result of *involun-tary ignorance*. We may want to do what is right, but we are mistaken in our facts. As I was working on this chapter, I was privileged to actually see how God enlightened a conscience with the truth. In Chicago I observed a meeting between a right-to-life organization and the newly appointed director of a Women's Studies Center in a Muslim country. This woman is not only a feminist, but she is one of the authors of her country's national report for the UN Conference on Women. Furthermore, she was going to Beijing as a voting delegate to the UN Conference. Her reason for meeting with the pro-life group was to learn their educational techniques. We were un-sure whether she was pro-life or pro-abortion. As the meeting began, the president of the pro-life organization gave a very concise, nonconfrontational explanation of the pro-life position. The Muslim woman enthusiastically agreed to view THE SI-LENT SCREAM video while she drank a cup of coffee and munched on a muffin. Within a few minutes into the film, she put her coffee down and stopped eating. Stunned by the video, she began interrupting the film with question after question. After viewing only 19 minutes of the film she told us that "I am very emotional over this. I had no idea that the baby's heartbeat began at 18 days. I must confess when I came to this meeting I was pro-choice. I did not know it was a baby before three months....I work with family planning programs in my country, what do I do now?" The woman was then put in touch with the Couple-to-Couple League to receive help in developing a natu-ral family planning (NFP) program for her country. This woman, a Muslim, saw the truth and is willing to act on it even through it could be professionally detrimental to her. Shown the truth, she corrected her false conscience.

What does *freedom of conscience* mean? This gets a bit sticky. Many people claim that they are following their consciences when they leave their spouses for someone else, sleep with someone, defraud their employer, or cheat in business matters. Politicians, who claim they are "personally opposed" to an evil but will not impose their views on the nation, are making a moral evil a legal right. A moral evil can never be a legal right. These people are not following natural law and have thereby deformed their con-sciences. They are choosing evil rather than good.

Pope John Paul II in *The Splendor of Truth* warns: "Certain currents of modern thought have gone so far as to exalt freedom to such an extent that it becomes an absolute, which would then be the source of values...Once the idea of a universal truth about the good, knowable by human reason, is lost, inevitably the notion of conscience also changes. Conscience is no longer considered...as an act of a person's intelligence, the function of which is to apply the universal knowledge of the good in a specific situation and thus to express a judgment about the right conduct to be chosen here and now. Instead, there is a tendency to grant to the individual conscience the prerogative of independently determining the criteria of good and evil and then acting accordingly. Such an outlook is quite congenial to an individualistic ethic, wherein each individual is faced with his own truth, different from the truth of others. Taken to its extreme consequences, this individualism leads to a denial of the very idea of human nature."[5]

The "freedom" extolled today is really license. St. Augustine points out: "The beginning of freedom is to be free from crimes...such as murder, adultery, fornication, theft, fraud, sacrilege, and so forth. Once one is without these crimes (and every Christian should be without them), one begins to lift up one's head toward freedom. But this is only the beginning of freedom, not perfect freedom."[6] The Holy Father adds: "Human freedom and God's law are not in opposition; on the contrary, they appeal one to the other. The follower of Christ knows that his vocation is freedom."[7]

All theoretical and practical attempts to build a system of morality not based on our own responsibility before God are futile. They cannot truly guide us toward a good and moral life. When the human being decides to be responsible only to himself or to his own conscience, or to society, mankind, history, or any other projection of himself, he soon finds ways to excuse his moral aberrations by silencing the voice of his own conscience, changing the laws, rewriting history, or adapting social conventions to justify his wrongdoing. The only victim of this

---

[5]*The Splendor of Truth,*op. cit., n.32.
[6]Cf. St. Augustine, *De Sermone Domini in Monte*, I, 1, 1: CCL 35,1-2.
[7]*The Splendor of Truth*, op.cit., n.17.

rationalization is the human person himself, who is left morally deformed and incapable of seeking God as the Supreme Good and the source of the person's eternal happiness.

To avoid this unfortunate situation, The ***Catechism of the Catholic Church*** insists: "Conscience must be informed and moral judgment enlightened. A well-formed conscience is upright and truthful....The education of conscience is indispensable for human beings who are subjected to negative influences and tempted by sin to prefer their own judgment and to reject authoritative teachings. The education of the conscience is a lifelong task."[8]

How To Develop A Well-Formed Conscience

How do we educate our conscience? It requires the knowledge of the laws and principles that govern moral life. These laws are contained in the Ten Commandments and in the Precepts of the Church. The Ten Commandments summarize the main precepts of the natural law. The Precepts of the Church are a summary of the main obligations proper to Christians. This is just the beginning of our education. Just as we cannot fit into the clothes we wore when we made our First Communion, our moral knowledge must expand beyond what we learned when we made our first confession, left Catholic grade school, high school, or college. Even more important than Bible study groups are groups that study Catholic doctrine and morality. We should take time to read each of the Holy Father's encyclicals. Yes, they may at times be deep, and slow reading, but with the guidance of the Holy Spirit, we can comprehend the points the Holy Father is teaching. The books written by Fr. John Hardon, SJ, explain the faith and morality very clearly and concisely. The ***Catechism of the Catholic Church*** should not only be a best seller, it should be read. It is easy reading and each chapter ends with a short summary. *The Faith Explained* by Leo Trese is another excellent book not only for Catholics, but also non-Catholics and teens. For those having difficulty finding time to read, there are excellent audio tapes available. There is no reason today for anyone in the U.S. to have a false conscience. The truth is readily available. It is just up to us to make

---

[8]*Catechism of the Catholic Church*, op. cit., n. 1783-1784.

the time and effort to seek the truth. Then we have to accept the truth and live it. St. Wilfrid of England warns, "You certainly sin if, having heard the decrees of the Apostolic See and of the universal Church, and having heard that the same things are confirmed in Holy Scripture, you refuse to follow them."

We also form our conscience through daily mental and vocal prayers, reading spiritual books, the lives of the saints, and the Bible. In addition, if we are seeking the truth, we should also be striving to live a virtuous life.

Spiritual direction in confession is an aid in correctly forming our conscience. We all have spiritual blind spots. A solid confessor can help us overcome this spiritual blindness. Since sanctifying grace and the gifts of the Holy Spirit are infused and strengthened in the soul through the sacraments, it follows that frequent sacramental confession contributes greatly to the formation of conscience. In fact, if the fulfillment of a particular moral obligation seems especially difficult or even impossible, a sincere confession will help to set the will straight and strengthen it in the right direction. The difficulty is not in the moral law, but in the wrong inclination of our will.

In order for us to use the Sacrament of Reconciliation in a manner that will benefit our souls, our consciences must be formed correctly. St. John Vianney, the Cure of Ars once said, "An ignorant person is like a dying man lying unconscious: he knows neither the malice of sin nor the beauty of grace nor the value of his soul. He goes from sin to sin, like a rag dragged through the mire."

This does not have to be the story of our lives. God's saving love is greater than our sins, but only if we recognize His truth and allow His grace to work within us.

CHAPTER 8

"Lord, That I May See!"

"The Peace one receives from confession depends on the priest."

True peace and joy come from the removal of our sins and the guilt that burdens our conscience. This does *not* depend on the personality or the holiness of the priest. It depends on Christ's merciful forgiveness first of all, and secondly, on our disposition of sorrow and repentance. Consider what Our Lord tells us through Blessed Faustina: "Come to the feet of My representative...I Myself am waiting there for you. I am only hidden by the priest...I myself act in your soul...Make your confession before Me. The person of the priest is, for Me, only a server. Never analyze what sort of a priest it is that I am making use of; open your soul in confession as you would to Me, and I will fill it with My light..."

John Paul II explains: "According to the most ancient traditional idea, the sacrament is a kind of juridical action; but this takes place before a tribunal of mercy rather than of strict and rigorous justice...namely insofar as sinners reveal their sins and their condition as creatures subject to sin; they commit themselves to renouncing and combating sin; accept the punishment (sacramental penance) which the confessor imposes on them and receive absolution from him...

"Whether as a tribunal of mercy or a place of spiritual heal-

103

ing, under both aspects the sacrament requires a knowledge of the sinner's heart in order to be able to judge and absolve, to cure and heal. Precisely for this reason the sacrament involves on the part of the penitent a sincere and complete confession of sins....["1]

In the Gospel of St. Mark we read about the blind man, Bartimaeus. He was sitting along the side of the road begging when he heard a commotion. When he learned from bystanders that Jesus was passing by, he grabbed this golden opportunity to seek help. Yelling over the huge crowd, he begged, "Son of David, have mercy on me!" Jesus, hearing his plea, called him forward and asked, "What would you have me do for you?" Bartimaeus instantly replied, "Lord, that I may see."[2]

This same plea should be ours as we prepare to make a good confession. Because of original sin, at times it is difficult for us to see our own sinful traits, habits, or lack of sorrow for sins committed.

How To Make A Good Confession

In order to receive the sacrament of Penance worthily there are five steps we should sincerely strive to fulfill. They are:

1. Examine our consciences well.
2. Be sorry for our sins.
3. Have a firm purpose not to commit the sin again.
4. Confess our sins to the priest.
5. Be willing to do the penance the priest gives us.

Let's briefly consider each of these steps.

The Examination Of Conscience

In the fabulous play "Phantom of the Opera," Christine tells the ghastly looking Phantom, your "haunted face holds no horror for me now...It's in your soul that the true distortion lies..."[3] Likewise, there is distortion within our souls. That is why it is important for us to develop the habit of examining our consciences well. Ronald Knox explains, "We are not, please God,

---

[1]*Reconciliation and Penance*, op. cit., n.31, III pp.77-79.
[2]Mark 10:51.
[3]George Perry, *The Complete Phantom of the Opera* (New York: Henry Holt and Company, 1991), p. 165.

blind as Bartimaeus was, but our spectacles have got a good deal furred over, haven't they? We don't see straight always; we mistake the things that aren't worth having, the things that aren't worth doing, for the things that are. And when He asks us what He can do for us, we still have to answer, 'Lord, give me back my sight! Give me back the clear sight I had when I was fresh from school, with all the influences of a Catholic training; give me back the clear sight I had when I was a new convert, and my way was all mapped out for me in black and white. Give me back the power to see things straight, as they really are!'"[4]

Confession is the time to take off our rose colored glasses and view ourselves as God sees us. The Holy Father, writes that the preparation for the Jubilee Year 2000, "demands of everyone an *examination of conscience....*"[5] He continues: "...[T]he Church....cannot cross the threshold of the new millennium without encouraging her children to purify themselves, through repentance of past errors and instances of infidelity, inconsistency, and slowness to act. Acknowledging the weaknesses of the past is an act of honesty and courage which helps us to strengthen our faith, which alerts us to face today's temptations and challenges and prepares us to meet them."[6]

"On the threshold of the new millennium Christians need to place themselves humbly before the Lord and examine themselves on *the responsibility which they too have for the evils of our day.*"[7]

In union with the Holy Father, let's seriously consider the examination of conscience. We lead such busy lives that at times it's difficult to remember what we did last week or even this past afternoon. Depending on the length of time between confessions, sometimes it's difficult to remember our sins unless they are blatantly mortal sins or embarrassing venial sins. For this reason it's helpful to develop the habit of doing a daily examination of conscience.

---

[4]Ronald Knox, *The Layman and His Conscience* (New York: Sheed & Ward, 1961), pp. 8-9.
[5]John Paul II, *Tertio Millenio Adveniente*, Apostolic Letter (Boston: St. Paul Books & Media, 1994), p.40.
[6]Ibid, p.38-39.
[7]Ibid, p.41.

There are actually two different types of examination of conscience—the general exam and the particular exam. The general examination of conscience considers all the sins and imperfections committed during a certain time period such as each day or during the time since one's last confession. The particular examination of conscience concerns our particular struggle with a certain vice or imperfection. We will consider the examination of conscience here in just a summary format. In the appendix of this book is a profile for doing an examination of conscience in depth.

The General Examination Of Conscience

Going over the day (or period), we can see the rough spots and the areas where we have to improve. Keep a little notebook and jot down in a form of code your failings for the day. This will help you to see a pattern where you have to struggle more. It will also help you to make a better and more complete confession. Consider the cause of your failings. Are you short of temper because you are tired? Maybe getting to bed earlier would help. If moodiness and sensitivity are the problem maybe pride is the root of unhappiness. By knowing this, it's easier to catch ourselves before we react to an imaginary slight or even real ones. If impure thoughts are a problem, avoiding TV, movies, and certain magazines may be the solution. If we tend to gossip with certain people, we can avoid that person, change the subject, or find an excuse to leave the situation.

Blessed Josemaría encourages us to "Apply a *savage* sincerity to your examination of conscience; that is to say, be courageous. It is the same as when you look at yourself in the mirror to know where you have hurt yourself or where the dirt is or where your blemishes are, so that you can get rid of them."[8] He goes on to say, "Here is a point for your daily examination. Have I allowed an hour to pass, without talking with my Father God? Have I talked to Him with the love of a son? You Can!"[9]

After the bookkeeping each night, resolve to improve in some small way the next day. What can you do to remind yourself to pray during the day? If your patience wears thin when

---

[8]Blessed Josemaría Escrivá, *Furrow* (New York: Scepter Press, 1987), #148.
[9]Ibid, #657.

the children come home from school or work pressure builds, resolve to prepare yourself spiritually before you reach that point by saying the rosary or reading the Gospel. It will help you to stay in control. The peace received from these pious practices will spill into your personality making you more relaxed and cheerful besides helping you to control your emotions.

Keep resolutions for the next day simple. If they become too grand, we become discouraged when they fall through. If a resolution does not work, then during the examination of conscience the next night consider another plan of action. Remember, conversion is a day to day process.

The general examination goes over not only our day, but also our interior life. Did we make an effort to try to get to daily Mass? Did we fit in some mental prayer, the rosary, spiritual reading, etc.? If not, why not? How can we fit them in the next day? This examination should not take more than a minute or two. The idea is not to become scrupulous by trying to see how terrible we are, but rather to see where we may be offending God and how we can improve in a practical way.

Another way to do the general examination is to consider: What good did I do today? What could I have done better? What did I omit that I should have done? How did I offend God? How did I show love of neighbor? How did I live family life (if married)?

The Particular Examination Of Conscience

The other examination we should do each evening is called the particular examination. In this exam we zero in on a specific area in which we have to struggle harder. It may be cheerfulness, patience, obedience, helpfulness, generosity, charity, temperance, humility, chastity, and so forth. These are the virtues that are opposed to the Seven Capital Sins in Chapter 4. By going over the capital sins we can detect the area where we personally need to improve. This is called our predominant fault. Fr. James McElhone points out: "A predominant fault is that fault which brings forth one's ordinary temptations, or that into which one is prone to fall, or into which one has fallen most frequently in the past."[10]

---

[10]James F. McElhone, C.S.C., *Particular Examen* (Harrison, NY: Roman Catholic Books: 1952), p.19

Once we see a particular sin cropping up regularly during our general examination of conscience, we can take that defect as our point of particular exam so that we can carefully check our progress. Each day there should be some improvement in the area of our personal struggle. We can overcome our predominant fault by practicing the virtue opposed to it such as humility which is opposed to pride, generosity which is opposed to avarice, charity which is opposed to envy, patience which is opposed to anger, chastity which is opposed to lust, temperance which is opposed to gluttony, order that is opposed to sloth. We can also practice our strongest virtue that is called the virtue of predilection. For example, some of us are kind by nature. Others are patient, generous, orderly, or thoughtful. By developing this virtue further, others develop along with it since all the virtues are interconnected. It may take months, even years, to overcome some defects but each day we should be striving in some concrete manner to conquer our particular weakness. Our particular exam may also be mentioned in confession so that the priest can help us work on this point of struggle.

St. Peter Julian Eymard writes: "In spite of the supreme importance of the examen, we do not like it. It is the most difficult and repugnant of the acts of piety. And why is that? Because we do not like to see ourselves always guilty, always humiliated. Moreover, we are very reluctant about recollecting ourselves in our thoughts, about analyzing and examining them...and yet, without the examen of conscience, self amendment is an impossibility; we cannot correct ourselves of what we are not aware.

"A pious soul who has given up examining herself is always living in extremes: either in a blind security...or in a false and exaggerated humility, because she does not want to take the trouble to see and state precisely to herself the truth of her condition. We think we have done well and said the last word when we have confessed before God and self that we are the poorest and most miserable of creatures and have repeated this same accusation in the tribunal of penance. The result? We remain always with the same defects and steadily decrease in piety."[11]

---

[11] St. Peter Julian Eymard, "Confession-A Means of Sanctification," Chapter VII, taken from *Thy Kingdom Come,* Volumn 97, No.1, p.23.

Preparation For Confession

As we prepare for our confession, we should begin with a prayer to the Holy Spirit for spiritual light and our guardian angel. Review the Ten Commandments, the Works of Mercy, and the Precepts of the Church. How did we offend God in these various areas? If we have been faithful in doing our daily spiritual bookkeeping, preparation should be easy for us. Our confession should not be a grocery list of sins that are the same each time we go. Instead, we have to go to the *root* of our sins to find the main cause of our turning away from God. If I talk excessively, is it out of pride, hunger for attention or nervousness? If I walk around with a chip on my shoulder, it is because of pride, anger, or envy? Only when we name the root that causes our sins can we be given helpful direction by our confessor. We will then be able to soar spiritually.

The Necessity Of Sorrow

For our sins to be forgiven, we *must* be sorry for them. So many times we hear people justify their actions with this flippant comment, "Oh, I'll just go to confession later." We cannot have the attitude that we can do whatever we please, as long as we eventually go to confession to be forgiven. To be forgiven, we have to be truly sorry that we committed the sin or sins. Each sin is an offense against God and must be taken seriously—even if it seems as if it is a "harmless white lie" or "light gossip." This sorrow comes from our heart and will rather than from the emotions. By meditating on the Agony, Suffering, and Death of our Lord, we can develop a horror of sin and true sorrow when we fall. "...[T]he essential act of penance, on the part of the penitent, is contrition, a clear and decisive rejection of the sin committed, together with a resolution not to commit it again, out of the love which one has for God and which is reborn with repentance. Understood in this way, contrition is therefore the beginning and the heart of conversion...which brings the person back to God like the prodigal son returning to his father... Hence 'upon this contrition of heart depends the truth of penance,'" writes John Paul II.[12]

------

[12]*Reconciliation and Penance*, op. cit., pp.79-80.

Without sorrow, we can go to the Sacrament of Reconciliation, confess our sins to the priest, do the penance, but our confession is merely going through the motions. Only when we are sorry is our confession valid.

There are two types of sorrow/contrition—imperfect contrition and perfect contrition. Imperfect contrition is sorrow for the sins we commit because they are ugly or we fear punishment (i.e. eternity in Hell). The Council of Trent explains that while imperfect contrition cannot obtain the forgiveness of grave (mortal) sins, it does dispose us to seek forgiveness in the Sacrament of Reconciliation[13]and is sufficient for obtaining God's forgiveness in Confession. When sorrow for our sins arises solely because we love God and deeply regret offending Him, this sorrow is called perfect contrition. The Council of Trent teaches that perfect contrition remits venial sins. It also obtains forgiveness of mortal sins if we have the firm resolution to go to confession as soon as possible.[14] All people outside the Catholic Church must have perfect contrition to have their mortal sins forgiven since most other religions do not have the Sacrament of Reconciliation.

"Sin No More"

To make a good confession, we have to have a firm purpose of amendment in our will. In other words, we sincerely want to strive not to sin in this way again. We cannot confess that we gossiped and then plan to continue gossiping. We cannot sincerely confess a lie without a willingness to work on being truthful and sincere. It would be a sham to confess that we saw a filthy movie or read a risqué book but intend to go and see another such film or read the same type of book in the future. We have to be sincere with God. That is why the particular examination is so important. It is this tool that helps us to avoid falling into the same sins over and over again.

Granted, as sinners we will probably commit the same sins again but at the time of confession, our wills should be set to avoid these sins as much as humanly possible.

---

[13]Cf. Council of Trent (1551): DS 1678; 1705.
[14]Cf. Council of Trent (1551): DS 1677.

God's Tribunal

"It's enough to tell just a couple of little sins to the priest. At these penance services, where a lot of people are waiting in line, I don't have to say my mortal sins. Besides, I'm embarrassed to do this."

Well, don't be. To make a valid confession and to receive forgiveness, we need to confess *all* of our unconfessed mortal sins to a priest who represents God, no matter how many people are waiting in line. It is not a case of just picking and choosing. "Nothing is more personal and intimate than this sacrament, in which the sinner stands alone before God with his sin, repentance and trust. No one can repent in his place or ask forgiveness of his sin. . . .Everything takes place between the individual alone and God,"[15] so states the Holy Father. It is a confirmation of the availability of God's mercy in return for our sincerity.

To make a good confession, we should strive to be humble and sincere. Remember the three C's. Our sins should be confessed clearly, concisely, and completely. If we are humble, we will not take up the priest's time by going into long, rambling stories as a way of excusing ourselves of the sins we committed. We should begin our confession with any and all mortal sins. It's best to get the biggest off our chest first! When we confess mortal sins, we are to tell their kind, the number of times committed,* and any circumstances changing their nature. Should we forget to confess a mortal sin, it is forgiven in confession but we must tell the sin in our next confession if it again comes to mind. If we knowingly conceal a mortal sin in confession, the sins we confess are not forgiven and we commit an additional mortal sin of sacrilege. Should we conceal a mortal sin in confession, the next time we go, we must explain about the sin, confess the rest of our sins, and mention the sacraments received since the bad confession.

Fear or embarrassment should never be part of our confession. We should never be afraid of telling a priest anything.

---

[15] *Ibid.*

* If for some reason we do not remember the exact number, it is sufficient to give an approximate number during the span of time when the sins were committed.

There is nothing that we can say that he has not heard before. We are protected by the seal of confession. The priest who hears our confession can never repeat to anyone anything that we confess. If we are embarrassed or unsure of how to confess a sin, we can ask the priest for help.

While it is necessary to confess every mortal sin, it is not necessary to confess venial sins, yet it is better to do so as explained in the earlier chapters. Tell the priest your particular exam and how your struggle is going. Ask for advice. When you complete your confession, you can also ask the priest for spiritual direction. Fr. Dubay describes spiritual direction as "the guiding of a person into a life truly under the dominion of the Holy Spirit, who is the primary director. It helps the directee to be more and more docile to the light and promptings of the divine Sanctifier, identifying impediments to this, as well as ways to overcome them, giving instruction and encouragement in living a life of virtue, and assisting the directee to advance on the path of prayer—the road to union with God."[16] By going to the same confessor frequently, he can help you to grow deeper in the love of God and in the avoidance of sin. Through the frequent contact with you in confession, he can more easily help you progress spiritually. Remember, you are permitted to take as much time in confession as you need. Do not rush or hurry through. If you have questions, feel free to ask the priest. Do not be intimidated by people waiting.

A Time For Penance

To complete the sacrament, we must be willing to perform the penance that the priest gives to us. The penance is a prayer or work given to us in order to make up for our sins. It helps to repair the harm caused by our fault, and to put us at one with God again. This is the meaning of atonement. We should accept our penance with gratitude, and fulfill it as soon as possible. In this way we show our prompt desire to make up for our sins.

At the same time, remember that the small penances given nowadays usually just begin to make reparation for our sins. If we do not make atonement or reparation on earth, we will have

---

[16]Thomas Dubay, S.M., *Seeking Spiritual Direction* (Ann Arbor, MI: Servant Publications, 1993), pp. 32-33.

to "do time"later in Purgatory. It is through our daily living, the acceptance of suffering and pain, through fasting, almsgiving, our Masses, and prayers that we make reparation for our sins on earth. We also do penance "by gestures of reconciliation, concern for the poor, the exercise and defense of justice and right, by the admission of faults to one's brethren, fraternal correction, revision of life, examination of conscience, spiritual direction, acceptance of suffering, and endurance of persecution for the sake of righteousness. Taking up one's cross each day and following Jesus is the surest way of penance."[17] Daily Mass "...is a remedy to free us from our daily faults and to preserve us from mortal sins. Reading Sacred Scripture, praying the Liturgy of the Hours and the Our Father—every sincere act of worship or devotion revives the spirit of conversion and repentance within us and contributes to the forgiveness of our sins. *The seasons and days of penance* in the course of the liturgical year (Lent, and each Friday in memory of the death of the Lord) are intense moments of the Church's penitential practice. These times are particularly appropriate for spiritual exercises, penitential liturgies, pilgrimages as signs of penance, voluntary self-denial such as fasting and almsgiving, and fraternal sharing (charitable and missionary works)."[18]

WHAT ARE MORTIFICATIONS?

The penance we receive in confession also helps us to develop a spirit of mortification. For those unfamiliar with this term, mortifications are sacrifices or acts of self-denial that are done out of love of God. They are often something that we would prefer not to do. In essence, mortification is the voluntary performance of an act that is not pleasant but necessary for our *spiritual* growth. Mortifications help us to develop dominion over our actions and the things of this world. When mortifications are connected with Our Lord's suffering, they also help to redeem the world. Blessed Josemaría Escrivá explains, "From every point of view, mortification has an extraordinary importance. Considering it humanly, anyone who does not know how to control himself will never be able to have a positive influence on others. He will be overwhelmed by his surroundings as soon

---

[17]*Catechism of the Catholic Church*, op. cit., n.1435.
[18]Ibid, n.1436-1438.

as he finds they appeal to his personal tastes. He will be a man without energy, incapable of any great effort when required.

"Considering it before God, do you not think it appropriate for us to show, with these small acts, how much we love, obey and respect the One who gave everything for us?"[19] He explains, "But I must remind you, mortification does not usually consist of great renunciations, for situations requiring great self-denial seldom occur. Mortification is made up of small conquests, such as smiling at those who annoy us, denying the body some superfluous fancy, getting accustomed to listening to others, making full use of the time God allots us. . .and so many other details. We find it in the apparently trifling problems, difficulties and worries which arise without our looking for them in the course of each day."[20]

Fr. Luna, in his booklet on confession, gives us concrete examples of mortifications that we can easily do. "Usually the best opportunities for penance are right at hand. . . work well done; punctuality; order in our personal effects; restraining a sharp tongue; overcoming anger; guarding our senses; understanding people with different tastes and opinions; small sacrifices at meals; getting up and going to bed on time; finishing what we are doing; putting things away; not being a pest; and not worrying over trifles; and so on. These ordinarily situations provide the best opportunity of mortifying ourselves and offering God this prayer of the body."[21]

Other mortifications include giving up a cocktail; not getting in the last word in a conversation; struggling to be cheerful; stifling complaints; not watching TV or listening to the radio; drinking water instead of coffee, tea, or pop; giving up snacks; putting the wishes of others before our own desires.

The Question Of Scruples

Some people are troubled by the spiritual suffering known as scruples. Fr. Alfred Wilson, CP defines a scruple as "'an uneasy and unfounded fear of having committed sin, based on feeling rather than on reason.' Scrupulosity is an obsession of

---

[19] *Furrow*, op. cit., n.980.
[20] *Christ Is Passing By*, op. cit., n. 37., n.37.
[21] Rev. F. Luna, *Making the Most of Confession* (New York: Scepter, 1974), pp. 12-13.

the moral conscience causing a state of acute anxiety."[22] Fr. Thomas Dubay elaborates: "Scrupulous people are sincere, but they are ruled more by fear than by love. Their fear is distorted: small things are seen as large, and unfounded worries about guilt torture the individual from morning until night."[23]

Scruples can be caused by physical, psychological or spiritual problems. "People are often afflicted with scruples when they are suffering from shock, or from strain and nervous exhaustion caused by overwork, adolescence, change of life, etc."[24] The scrupulous person, while wanting to do everything right, sees himself or herself doing everything wrong. Sometimes, scruples are caused by focusing too much on ourselves. If we are busy doing God's work, rather than our own, scruples should diminish. We won't have time to think about ourselves since we are too busy doing good! The scrupulous person is also unsure of the mercy and forgiveness of God. But we must trust Him in this matter. For the sincere, He is a God of mercy, and we need to try to put everything in His hands. God reads our hearts and knows when we sincerely are trying to do what is right. By repeating the aspirations, "Most Sacred Heart of Jesus, grant me peace" or "I abandon everything into thy most Sacred Heart," over and over again when we are besieged with scruples, we can develop a deeper trust in God. Fr. Wilson also recommends developing the virtues of hope, charity, and a good sense of humor. Don't confuse your conscience with that nagging voice that drives you crazy. Finally, practice absolute obedience to your confessor. Don't second guess him or ignore his advice. It comes from God.

Another area of concern for the scrupulous is what is said in confession. Did I say it right, or forget part of the details? Occasionally it may help to write out clearly, concisely, and completely the points of concern. Read to the priest what you have written so nothing is left out to trouble you later. (Bring a small flashlight along if there is no light in the confessional.) This will guarantee that you covered everything. This practice should

[22]Alfred Wilson, CP, *Pardon and Peace* (Garden City, NY: Image Books, 1965), p. 148.
[23]*Seeking Spiritual Direction*, op. cit., p.69.
[24]*Pardon and Peace*, op. city. p.149.

not become a habit, however. Another way to handle this problem is to explain to the priest you are scrupulous, and then mentioned the commandments you sinned against. Explain to the priest that he can question you about any violated commandment. Then follow the guidance and direction of the priest.

As you prepare for confession, tell Our Lord how sorry you are for your sins. Once the confession is over, be assured that God is pleased with you and your confession, your sorrow was adequate, and the confession was complete. Then mortify your memory and imagination. Cut any thoughts about past confessions that you fear might be invalid. Trust in the mercy of God and accept His forgiveness. God has forgiven you. Now it is time to forget and go on with life!

Confusion over the difference between a temptation and a sin can also cause scruples. Was it a sin or just a temptation? To be a sin, we have to give our consent; for there to be grave sin there must be full knowledge and full consent. A thought that comes to mind, if not willed, accepted, or enjoyed, is *not* a sin. Many times the "sins" that are bothering us are acts of nature that are unwanted and unplanned motions of our lower appetites. One priest explained that a gross thought could even tempt us in the Communion line. It's like bird droppings. You do not will it but it happens. Shoo the thought or temptation away as you would a mosquito or fly. Say aspirations, get busy working (when this is possible), and the temptation will pass. If you are unsure if something is a sin, ask the priest in confession. There are also acts of nature such as pangs of jealousy or envy, angry facial expressions, even sexual stimulation that are not willed. These are not sins as long as we do not consent to them.

Spiritual writer Jack McArdle leaves us with this profound thought about the effects of confession: "When the Father looks at me He sees the image of His Son—but it takes a great deal of chipping away and sandpaper treatment to produce the masterpiece."[25] It's the Sacrament of Reconciliation that does that work to produce the masterpiece within our souls.

---

[25]Jack McArdle, "Holiness," *The Voice Of Padre Pio* Magazine (San Giovanni Rotondo, Italy: Our Lady of Grace Capuchin Friary), Vol. XVIII, #4, 1988, p.11.

CHAPTER 9

"May God Give You Pardon and Peace"

"The priests are available very little for confessions. I don't want to trouble father by calling and making an appointment."

During a homily in San Antonio, Texas, John Paul II stressed that "the ministry of reconciliation is a fundamental part of the Church's life and mission...[I]t is important for me to emphasize that it is above all in the Sacrament of forgiveness and reconciliation that the power of the redeeming blood of Christ is made effective in our personal lives...

"Again I ask all my brother Bishops and priests to do everything possible to make the administration of this Sacrament *a primary aspect* of their service to God's people. There can be no substitute for the means of grace which Christ Himself has placed in our hands. The Second Vatican Council *never* intended that this Sacrament of Penance be less practiced; what the Council expressly asked for was that the faithful might more easily understand the sacramental signs and more eagerly and *frequently* have recourse to the sacraments."[1]

Do not be embarrassed to call and make an appointment for confession if your parish does not regularly schedule them. Or, if they are scheduled but you are unable to go because of time conflict, do call and make alternate plans with your parish

---

[1]Press release from the Sept. 13, 1987 Homily at San Antonio Eucharist (Westover Hills).

117

priest. By doing so, you will actually help your pastor and parish priests to fulfill their priestly ministry. Remember, God primarily judges priests not by the paperwork they completed or the meetings they attended, but by the souls they brought closer to Him through the ministry of the sacraments and spiritual direction. Should you feel reluctant to ask, consult the **Catechism of the Catholic Church** which states: "Priests must encourage the faithful to come to the sacrament of penance and must make themselves available to celebrate this sacrament each time Christians reasonably ask for it."[2]

Should you run into a situation in which the priest is unwilling or unable to accommodate you, call a convent, monastery, or Catholic retirement home and ask about the availability of confessions. Another possibility is to ask a retired priest if he would be willing to become your confessor.

"Last Saturday I went to confession face to face. I was ashamed to say a sin against chastity that I committed. I'm sure that God will understand. Confession behind the screen is pre-Vatican II."

These are probably common concerns but as discussed in the previous chapter, all mortal sins must be confessed, even if we are embarrassed to say them. If we hold a mortal sin back out of fear or embarrassment, we commit an additional mortal sin of sacrilege and our confession is invalid. To avoid such a situation, use a confessional that has a screen. We have the right to confess our sins either behind a screen or face-to-face. Contrary to what some people believe, confession behind the screen is not pre-Vatican II. This right is protected by canon law.[3] Monsignor G. B. Torello explains: "A confessional constructed in this way—required, according to current canon law, in all churches and oratories in an open and accessible place—protects the sacred character of the Sacrament of Reconciliation, while avoiding any reduction to the merely 'human,' which could threaten or even damage the freedom of the two people involved."[4] He continued by stressing: "Moreover, the use of the confessional fosters

[2]*Catechism of the Catholic Church*, op. cit., n.1464.
[3]Codex Iuris Canonici, can. 964 #2.
[4]Monsignor G.B. Torello, Ph.D., "Apologia For A Piece Of Church Furniture," *Homiletic & Pastoral Review*, Feb. 1994, p.47.

brevity....It helps the penitent to get down to essentials, avoiding a 'chattiness' that could occasion misuse of the sacrament, and not infrequently impatience or even scandal...."[5]

While many people may prefer the option of going to confession face-to-face, other laity and priests tend to agree with Msgr. Torello that "Face-to-face confession entails the danger of emotional involvement, which harms the seriousness and supernatural character of the sacramental action....We still have to recognize that the dividing wall and fixed screen protect modesty, guard against glances and guarantee a prudent distance between confessor and penitent."[6]

"It's been so long since the last time I went to confession. With all the changes, I'm not sure what to do."

Presently there are three rites that are used for the Sacrament of Reconciliation. The first is the rite we are all familiar with. John Paul II insists: "The first form—reconciliation of individual penitents—is the only normal and ordinary way of celebrating the sacrament, and it cannot and must not be allowed to fall into disuse or be neglected."[7] For those who put off going to confession because they do not know the new rite, below is the form to use. It is quite simple and similar to the way we were taught as children. Should you find that the priest uses a different response or formula, do not be concerned. There are several acceptable formats and he will gladly help you through your confession.

HOW TO GO TO CONFESSION ACCORDING TO THE NEW RITE OF PENANCE

1. Priest welcomes you as you enter the confessional. "May you receive the grace to make a good confession." Or, "I welcome you in the name of Christ."
   You: Make the sign of the Cross: "In the name of the Father, and of the Son, and of the Holy Spirit. Amen."
2. Priest says: "May God, who has enlightened every heart, help you to know your sins and trust in His mercy."
   You: (If you wish, read some passage from Sacred Scripture.)

---

[5]Ibid, p.48.
[6]Ibid.
[7]*Reconciliation and Penance*, op. cit., n.32.

3. You: Begin your confession: "Bless me: Father, for I have sinned. It has been _____ since my last confession. These are my sins: (Begin with any mortal sins. Tell your sins, the number of times, any necessary circumstances, even the roots of sin. If there are no mortal sins, confess some venial sins)" Then say: "For these and all the sins of my life, especially for _____ I am sorry." (At this point say in general any past sins you are particularly sorry for such as sins against charity, purity, etc.)

   Listen to any advice the priest gives to you. Accept the penance the priest gives. It will diminish the temporal punishment due to your sins.

4. You: Make your Act of Contrition (after the priest gives you any advice and your penance): "O, my God, I am heartily sorry for having offended you, and I detest all my sins because I dread the loss of heaven and the pains of hell; but most of all, because they offend you, my God, who are all-good and deserving of all my love. I firmly resolve, with the help of your grace, to confess my sins, do penance, and to amend my life amen."

   Or: use your own words of sorrow or a text of scripture, e.g., "Lord Jesus, Son of God, have mercy on me, a sinner." (Lk 18:13)

   At the same time as you are saying the Act of Contrition, the priest will be saying: "God, the Father of mercies, through the death and resurrection of His Son has reconciled the world to Himself and sent the Holy Spirit among us for the forgiveness of sins: through the ministry of the Church may God give you pardon and peace, and I absolve you from your sins, in the name of the Father, the Son, and the Holy Spirit."

   You respond, "Amen."

5. Praise to God and Dismissal of the penitent.
   Priest: "Give thanks to the Lord, for He is good."
   You say: "His mercy endures forever."
   Priest: "The Lord has freed you from your sins. Go in peace."
   You say: "Thank you, Father."

Following your confession, promptly and devoutly fulfill the penance given by the priest. If you still find going to confession intimidating, bring along this form and follow it during your confession.

The second form of the rite of confession focuses more on the community aspects of the sacrament. It is a penance service that includes prayers, specific readings, and a homily designed to help penitents examine their consciences and to prepare for their *individual* confessions. Prior to making one's individual confession, the group prays together "I confess to almighty God...," sings a hymn and ends with the Our Father. Then the penitents disburse to individual priests for their private confession. When all confessions have been completed, the priest invites all to thank God for this grace, and he encourages the penitents to do good works. A psalm is recited or a hymn sung followed by a prayer of thanksgiving and general dismissal.

John Paul II in speaking of the second form of celebration stated that because of its specific dimension certain aspects are of great importance: "The word of God listened to in common has a remarkable effect as compared to its individual reading and better emphasizes the ecclesial character of conversion and reconciliation. It is particularly meaningful at various seasons of the liturgical year and in connection with events of special pastoral importance. The only point that needs mentioning here is that for celebrating the second form there should be an adequate number of confessors present."[8]

The third form of the rite is general absolution. This could be used in case of danger of death, and where there is not time for the priest or priests to hear confessions of individual penitents such as war or other disasters. It can also be given if there are not enough confessors available to hear individual confessions, and the people through no fault of their own would be deprived of God's grace and Holy Communion for a long period of time.[9] John Paul II cautions: "The third form however—reconciliation of a number of penitents with general confession and absolution—is exceptional in character. It is therefore not left to free choice but is regulated by a special discipline."[10]

"While it is true that, when the conditions required by canonical discipline occur, use may be made of the third form of celebration, it must not be forgotten that this form cannot become an ordinary one, and it cannot and must not be used...except 'in cases of grave necessity.'....The exceptional

[8]Ibid. n.32
[9]See Canon 961, #2 in Code of Canon Law
[10]*Reconciliation and Penance*, op. cit., n.32.

use of the third form...must never lead to a lesser regard for, still less an abandonment of, the ordinary forms nor must it lead to this form being considered an alternative to the other two forms. It is not in fact left to the freedom of pastors and the faithful to choose from among these forms the one considered most suitable. It remains the obligation of pastors to facilitate for the faithful the practice of integral and individual confession of sins, which constitutes for them not only a duty but also an inviolable and inalienable right, besides being something needed by the soul."[11]

In the case of grave necessity, if the third form is used, the priest explains to the penitents that they must be properly disposed, they should repent of their sins, and have a firm purpose not to commit them again. Penitents are also told they are to repair any scandal or harm they have done. A penance is then given to the group. After receiving general absolution, it is the obligation of the penitent to explain to the priest at his or her next confession that general confession was received and disclose any mortal sins forgiven at that general confession. In any case, individual confession is the standard and accepted practice used by the Church, not general absolution.

Back On Track

Personal sin is a reality that is tearing apart our world and destroying peace in people's lives. The sins of mankind are reflected in the newspaper, radio, and evening TV news. If we examine our consciences we will see it in ourselves also—in our thoughts, words, actions, and omissions. I see its beginnings in my fourteen-month-old grandson who grabs his father's hair and yanks it when his Dad pulls him away from something he should not be doing. As we hit the senior years, if we have not struggled to overcome our defects and vices, they become magnified and our loneliness can turn to self-centeredness. Peace depends on our cooperation within the Sacrament of Reconciliation.

John Paul II insists: "...[I]t must be emphasized that the most precious result of the forgiveness obtained in the Sacrament of Penance consists in reconciliation with God...The forgiven

---

[11]Ibid, n.33.

penitent is reconciled with himself in his inmost being, where he regains his own true identity. He is reconciled with his brethren whom he has in some way attacked and wounded. He is reconciled with the Church. He is reconciled with all creation."[12]

To restore peace in our souls, in our relationships, and in our world, Catholics must return to the practice of frequent confession. It is only there that we can have our guilt forgiven and the rupture between God and ourselves repaired. It is only in the Sacrament of Penance that we receive the sacramental grace to help us overcome our tendencies toward particular sins. It is also in the confessional that God infuses into our souls an increase of sanctifying grace (God's life within us) which perfects our personality and helps us in turn to grow in the various virtues. As we grow in grace and goodness, our example positively influences our marriage, family life, professional work, and all other relationships. For Americans who expect an instant solution to problems, what faster road to peace and individual serenity is there than a few minutes once a week in the confessional?

The Sacrament of Penance is a sacrament of divine Love. In a vision granted to her, Sister Josefa Menendez claims that Our Lord revealed: "I love those who after a first fall come to me for pardon. . . .I love them still more when they beg pardon for their second sin, and should this happen again, I do not say a million times but a million million times, I still love them and pardon them, and I will wash in my Blood their last as fully as their first sin.

"Never shall I weary of repentant sinners, nor cease from hoping for their return, and the greater their distress, the greater my welcome. Does not a father love a sick child with special affection? Are not his care and solicitude greater? So is the tenderness and compassion of my Heart more abundant for sinners than for the just."[13]

Blessed Josemaría Escrivá, Founder of Opus Dei, who did so much to promote the use of this great sacrament in the years after the Second Vatican Council, expresses the joy that comes

---

[12]*Reconciliation and Penance*, op. cit., n.31, V.
[13]Sister Josefa Menendez, *I Wait For You, Selections from the Way of Divine Love* (Rockford, IL: Tan Books, 1985), p. 29.

from a good confession in terms of coming home again: "God is waiting for us...with open arms, even though we don't deserve it. It doesn't matter how great our debt is. Just like the prodigal son, all we have to do is open our heart, to be homesick for our Father's house, to wonder at and rejoice in the gift which God makes us of being able to call ourselves His children, of really being His children, even though our response to Him has been so poor."[14]

[14]Blessed Josemaría Escrivá de Balaguer, *Christ is Passing By* (New York: Scepter, 1982), n.64.

CHAPTER 10

The Power of Grace Within Our Soul

Have you read the lives of Sts. Elizabeth Seton, Catherine of Siena, Thomas More or Maximilian Kolbe? If you have, perhaps you thrilled to their daring, courage, fortitude and sporting spirits. Although we may be impressed by their love of God and their heroism, we seldom see the correlation between our lives and theirs. Do we realize that we have the same potential for greatness that they had? The only likely difference between the saints and us is that they cooperated completely with the grace and gifts of God—we are still struggling in this regard.

Though this book has been concerned with the Sacrament of Reconciliation, it seems worthwhile to finish with a general reflection about the life of grace and virtue, always keeping in mind our real purpose in life: *to be conformed as completely as possible to Christ our Savior.* These ideas also form the basis of Part III of the *Catechism of the Catholic Church*, and can help us appreciate the Sacrament of Confession even more within that context.

Through the sacrament of baptism we receive a divine quality that is called sanctifying grace. Grace does not change our nature, but takes whatever is good in it and transforms it: our intellect, our free will, our good habits or natural qualities are elevated and directed to for a supernatural purpose—our sanctification.

To better understand this concept, consider for a moment a dried-up sponge. It is rough to the touch and very light. The sponge's rigid and rough form makes its use impossible. For all practical purposes, it's worthless. Yet when you submerge the sponge in water, the water flows into its pores, giving the sponge weight and substance, manageability and usefulness.

Without God's grace we are like the dried-up sponge— rough, rigid, without purpose. Sanctifying grace penetrates our very nature, transforming it and enabling us to do acts that will lead us to heaven and prepare us to enjoy the Beatific Vision.

What is Sanctifying Grace?

Theologians explain that there are two different types of divine grace. One is called *sanctifying grace* and the other is called *actual grace*. The first is a permanent quality granted to the soul; the second is a transient help. Both types of grace are gifts from God. As human beings, we are not entitled to grace— grace is a gift over and above our nature, much the same as a college education is above the nature of a dog. That's why we label this grace "supernatural"—above nature.

Grace is an invisible, interior quality of our souls. Just as we cannot visually see our heart function, the fact that we are alive proves that it must be working. Likewise, the fact that we lift our minds and hearts to God throughout the day, struggle to do good and avoid evil and long to be close to God affirms the existence of God and his grace. Just as marriage unites a man and a woman, grace unites our souls to God.

Sanctifying grace is a permanent gift that can only be lost through mortal sin. Yet, in God's great love and mercy for us, it can be regained through the Sacrament of Penance or Reconciliation.

Sanctifying grace permeates all our faculties, making us pure and pleasing to God, just as the sun penetrates and warms the earth in the spring in order to bring forth lush growth in the summer and a rich harvest in the fall. This incredible gift of grace makes us temples of the Holy Spirit. This is what gives us our great dignity. This concept is in opposition to the world's idea that dignity rests on a person's social position, wealth, political power, or prestige in business.

Besides the wondrous gift of the indwelling of the Holy Spirit, sanctifying grace forms another special relationship between God and us. St. John explains: *"We are now sons of God"* (1 Jn 3:1).

Our adoption by God through sanctifying grace is more perfect than any human adoption. God's adoption is complete. We become brothers and sisters of Jesus Christ, the Son of God by nature, who is then our model: the one we should imitate; the one to whom we should be united by faith, hope and love, that we may be holy as the heavenly Father is holy (Mt 5:48). In other words, because of these loving gifts from our Father God, *we are not only called to be saints...we can truly become saints!*

To help us behave as His children, God lavishes on us certain supernatural virtues, along with the Gifts of the Holy Spirit so that we can live an intimate life with Him.

The Infused Virtues

Just for a moment, let us consider the three *infused theological virtues*, faith, hope and charity, which we receive with sanctifying grace. Just how do these virtues work within our souls?

Let's begin first with *faith.* By faith we come to participate in God's wisdom, for faith is "the virtue by which we firmly assent to all the truths God has revealed, on the word of God revealing them, who can neither deceive nor be deceived."[1] To firmly believe means that we have to accept God's word as true. We accept the findings of science that all matter is composed of atoms, yet we have never seen an atom. Our belief is based on the credibility of scientists. They could be mistaken. Unlike mortals, God is never mistaken because "He can neither deceive nor be deceived."

Our faith must be complete. We are to accept *all* the truths that God has revealed rather than pick and choose, according to

---

[1] Leo J. Trese, *The Faith Explained* (Chicago: Fides Publishers Association, 1959), p. 126.

our taste. We cannot say, "I believe in the Holy Eucharist but not in confession." Or, "I believe in heaven but not in purgatory or hell." When we pick and choose, we are in effect, saying that God is imperfect, that He can err.

We practice the virtue of faith when we make the effort to know the Lord's teachings, accept them, practice them, understand what and why we believe. We also practice it by making acts of faith, by receiving the sacraments and by praying. Fr. Hardon encourages us to associate with people who have a deep faith and to read authors who are loyal to the teaching authority of the Catholic Church. Reading authors who challenge the authority of the Church can kill our faith, just as drinking poison can kill our bodies.

By *hope* we come to participate in God's happiness, for hope is "the virtue by which we firmly trust that God, who is all-powerful and faithful to his promises, will in His mercy give us eternal happiness and the means to obtain it." The only way that we can lose heaven is through our own fault. God gives us the means. We have only to cooperate with the graces He gives to us daily. Fr. Leo Trese explains: "We do not fall into a black mood of despondency when 'things go wrong.' When our plans are upset, our expectations thwarted and failure seems to dog our every step, we know that in some way God is working this all out to our ultimate good."[2]

He goes on to say:

"It is this same trust in God's providence that comes to our aid when we are tempted to think that we are smarter than God; that we know better than He, under these circumstances, what is best for us. 'Maybe it is a sin, but we just can't afford another baby'; 'Maybe it isn't quite honest, but I've got to stay in business'; 'I know it seems a bit crooked, but politics are like that.' It is when alibis like these start to rise to our lips that we beat them down with our trust in God's providence. 'It looks as if doing the right thing is going to be rough on me,' we say, 'but God knows all the circumstances. He's smarter than I am. And He cares. I'll string along with Him.'"[3]

---

[2] Ibid., p. 127.
[3] Ibid., p. 128.

The virtue of hope is also practiced with frequent acts of hope, particularly during times of discouragement.

By *charity* we come to participate in God's love: it is "the virtue by which we love God above all things for His own sake, and our neighbor as ourselves for the love of God." Today it seems to be in vogue to talk about loving God. *We have so many people talking about loving God but few doing the actual loving!*

In order to love God above ourselves, we need God's help. "It is by the divine life within us that we are able to love God adequately, proportionately, with a love that is worthy of God...with a love also that is pleasing to God...."[4] It's like a college coed who calls home to ask her mother to pick up a gift at the store for Father's Day for her father. She concludes by saying, "I'll send you a check for the amount." The mother tells her daughter not to bother with the check. Why? Because the money comes from the same source, the family income. Our love toward God comes from God, the source of all love.

Fr. Hardon tells us that we sin against charity, "by failure to make acts of love of God, by inordinate love of creatures, by ungrateful murmurings against God, by a dislike or hatred of God, and by every sin committed, especially mortal sin."[5] If we love God above all things, we are willing to lose everything and anything rather than offend him.

Another group of treasures we receive with sanctifying grace are the infused moral virtues of prudence, justice, fortitude and temperance. They perfect and elevate the cardinal virtues or "hinge" virtues on which all the other virtues (good habits) hang. The infused moral virtues help us to direct all our good actions toward God. For example, when we exercise natural or human prudence, we choose the best course, among many, to attain a certain natural good. When we exercise supernatural or *infused prudence*, we choose the best course to do *God's* will in the matter. And the same can be said of the other infused moral virtues.

---

[4]Ibid., p. 128.

[5]John A. Hardon, SJ, *The Question and Answer Catholic Catechism* (New York: Doubleday & Company, Inc., 1981), p. 177.

With *infused justice*, we render to others what is due to them because the others are also God's creatures and so we become more like Him. We become more attuned to and strive for justice for the sake of God in all the situations we come across.

Infused fortitude helps us to endure struggles and trials, to be strong and steadfast in our goal to become saints. In situations in which we have no control, we learn to abandon ourselves to the will of God. We fight discouragement when we persevere in seemingly hopeless situations. Our desire to conform, to belong, to be "one of the crowd," the fear of public opinion, the fear of being criticized or ridiculed can interfere with the operation of fortitude.

Infused temperance controls our pleasure drive and brings it under control also for the sake of sanctity. According to Fr. Tanquerey,[6] we must remember that these infused virtues endow us, not with the facility, but with the possibility of converting our acts into acts that are worthy of God; that is, supernatural acts. In order to acquire that facility of action, we need the acquired natural moral virtues we acquire through the repetition of good acts. While our natural virtues become stronger through repetitive acts, the infused virtues of prudence, justice, temperance and fortitude grow through each new gift of sanctifying grace.

The infused moral virtues are lost when we commit a mortal sin but regained through sacramental confession. To help us better understand how the natural and the infused virtues work, let's consider the person with a drinking problem. If he becomes drunk, he loses the infused moral virtues, among them temperance, because of his sin. Through the sincere confession of his sin in the Sacrament of Reconciliation, he regains the infused virtues but in order to stay sober, he must acquire the natural virtue of temperance. If we do not have the acquired virtues, the infused moral virtues normally cannot be effective.

Through sanctifying grace, the Holy Spirit acts within the soul of the Christian as our Lord promised to His followers.

---

[6] Adolphe Tanquerey, SS, DD, *The Spiritual Life—A Treatise on Ascetical and Mystical Theology* (Belgium: Desclee & Company, 1930), p. 64, n.121.

Christian doctrine teaches that for the Holy Spirit to act in the soul, the soul needs new powers or potential abilities. These powers or abilities are called the Gifts of the Holy Spirit. In addition to the theological and infused moral virtues, we receive the Gifts of the Holy Spirit at Baptism. The Gifts are strengthened at Confirmation. They include wisdom, understanding, counsel, fortitude, knowledge, piety, and fear of the Lord. These gifts are to help us perfect the exercise of the virtues. Fr. Tanquerey explains that these gifts, conferred by sanctifying grace together with the infused virtues, do not exert a frequent or an intensive action except in souls who have acquired that supernatural docility and ease that render them completely obedient to the inspirations of the Holy Spirit. The Gifts of the Holy Spirit are new powers or potential abilities that allow the intellect and the will to be moved by the power of the Holy Spirit and to accomplish acts not expected from their natural constitution. We should not think that the action of the Holy Spirit in the soul is something out of the ordinary and accompanied with spectacular events. The motions of the Holy Spirit are certainly supernatural, but they are part of the ordinary and hidden work of God within the human soul.

Let's briefly review the Gifts of the Holy Spirit: *wisdom,* or the power to be moved by the Holy Spirit to judge about divine things; *understanding*, or power to be moved by the Holy Spirit to grasp revealed truths in a direct and immediate way—that is, not through ordinary rational process; *counsel*, or power to judge about particulars as they refer directly or indirectly to God, under the motion of the Holy Spirit; *fortitude,* or power to be moved by the Holy Spirit to resist fear in the face of danger; *knowledge,* or power to judge, under the motion of the Holy Spirit, about created things as they refer to God; *piety,* or power to behave as children of God and brothers of Christ, under the action of the Holy Spirit; *fear of God*, or power to resist evil, under the action of the Holy Spirit, out of fear of offending God because of His just punishments, and most of all, because of His goodness.

These are the powers that reside in the soul of the Christian in the state of grace and that the Holy Spirit uses to move us to do the kind of good that is beyond any natural expectation. What is required on our part, however, is our sincere willingness to be moved; that is, our docile response to God's promptings, and to be in His graces.

The action of the Holy Spirit in the soul cannot be known or measured by emotional experiences or by unusual happenings. In fact, it is a dangerous error to attempt to do so. This action is to be tested not by personal feelings but by objective signs. The first sign that a person is truly responding to the promptings of the Holy Spirit is his strict adherence to the doctrine of the Church. The second sign is obedience to legitimate superiors. The third sign, frequent reception of the sacraments, which are the main sources of sanctifying grace, provides a further guarantee for us of an authentic Christian life. The fourth sign, the practice of heroic virtue is the final test of authenticity.

Christian life aims at a growing identification with Christ, even to the point where the life of Christ is reproduced within the soul of each Christian. This cannot be achieved without God's action, that is to say, without the Holy Spirit, who fashions a person's life after the model that is Christ. The Gifts of the Holy Spirit are granted to the Christian for this very purpose: that a person may reach perfect identification with Christ.

From what we have just discussed, we can see that sanctifying grace is more than a vague theological term. Sanctifying grace affects our souls and our thoughts, desires and actions in very specific ways through the infused virtues and the Gifts of the Holy Spirit.

What About Actual Grace?

Actual grace is a spiritual help which God sends us in a particular circumstance (which choice to make); at a particular moment (such as at the moment of temptation); in a tricky situation where prudence and wisdom are required; or as an impulse to perform some good action.

Actual grace acts on our mind and will to set us in motion so that we can do supernatural acts. Interestingly, actual grace exerts its influence on us both in a moral and physical manner. It works on our souls in a moral manner through persuasion and attraction. We may be attracted to go to morning Mass during the week or persuaded to turn off a risqué TV show. Maybe we find ourselves going to confession when it wasn't in our schedule. These actions were prompted by actual grace.

Physically, actual grace adds new forces to our faculties that may be too weak to act by themselves. For instance, continuing to work/pray though we are exhausted. It may act by producing in our souls impulses to do good. Have you ever volunteered to do something and then wondered how in the world you had gotten yourself into such a position? It was actual grace that caused that impulse to do good such as watching a friend's children, driving a sick neighbor to the hospital, inviting people you dislike over for lunch, giving spiritual information to a group, lobbying your congressman for right-to-life legislation, making a meal for a shut-in, helping a fellow worker with his task. Interestingly, actual grace is necessary for the performance of every single supernatural act.

Sacramental Grace

There are sacramental graces proper to and given by each sacrament. To receive as much sacramental grace as possible, spiritually prepare well for the reception of each sacrament. For example, each time we go to confession there is a new infusion of divine life in us, more or less intense, depending on our disposition for receiving the sacrament. That is why it is so important to prepare ourselves when we go to confession. The sacramental graces we receive in confession help us to avoid committing in the future the sins we confessed. If a certain sin has become a bad habit (vice), the grace will help us fight the bad habit. If the habit is deeply ingrained, it may take a while, even years, for us working with grace to overcome it. This shouldn't discourage us. All God asks is that we sincerely try.

How Can We Grow in Grace?

Since grace is necessary for our sanctification, we can grow in sanctifying grace by receiving the sacraments. Sanctifying grace, as we mentioned before, can be lost through the committing of a mortal sin but we can regain sanctifying grace as soon as we make a good confession.

Actual grace works by persuading or attracting us to attend frequent Mass and receive Holy Communion often, thereby moving us to grow in sanctifying grace. By leading us to prepare well before Mass, actual grace helps us receive a greater increase of sanctifying grace from the Holy Eucharist. Actual grace also helps us grow in sanctifying grace by encouraging us to struggle every moment of the day to live for God and to do His will.

We can obtain actual graces through prayer and meritorious acts. The more faithful we are in cooperating with actual graces received, the more graces God will grant us. It is important to understand that we cannot merit grace on our own. It is purely a gift from God.

Grace is a mysterious power. We can neither feel, see, nor touch it, although we may sense its effects. While we may receive the sacraments often, we may appear to ourselves and to others to have many defects. Yet, if we are cooperating with God's grace, there is growth even if others and we are not aware of it. At other times, we can see the result of grace in the actions and behavior of those around us—for example, when a timid person displays great courage in standing up for God before others, or when an impatient person displays great compassion toward a person with a difficult temperament.

Since sanctification (holiness) is our ultimate goal, all of our actions should be measured by how they bring us closer toward this goal. Vatican II clearly explains that *sanctification is a moral obligation for everyone*, not just for the pious gentleman in the third row at daily Mass. In *Lumen Gentium*, we read:

"The Lord Jesus, the divine Teacher and Model of all perfection, preached holiness of life to each and every one of his disciples, regardless of their situation.....

"Thus it is evident to everyone that all the faithful of Christ of whatever rank or status are called to the fullness of the Christian life and to the perfection of charity. By this holiness a more human way of life is promoted even in this earthly society. In this way they can follow in his footsteps and mold themselves in his image, seeking the will of the Father in all things, devoting themselves with all their being to the glory of God and the service of their neighbor. In this way too, the holiness of the People of God will grow into an abundant harvest of good, as is brilliantly proved by the lives of so many saints in Church history."[7]

---

[7] Vatican II, *Lumen Gentium*, n.40

This call to holiness probably comes as a surprise. Many people feel that our total identification with Christ, when convenient, is praiseworthy but not obligatory. Some feel that God is a good friend to have as long as He doesn't complicate their lives. These errors ignore the express will of God who wills our sanctification (1 Thess. 4:3). These people ignore the whole purpose of "sanctifying" grace which God gives us so generously.

In a word, *to become a saint is the real purpose of our lives. It is something which we must earnestly desire and work toward.* When we deliberately refuse to make the effort of corresponding with the grace of God by avoiding a greater identification with Him for the sake of personal comfort and convenience, we become lukewarm. When we become lukewarm, grace rolls off us rather than soaking into our souls. Examples? God is constantly drawing us to Him in many ways such as through the sacraments, Mass and Holy Communion, retreats, doctrinal classes and spiritual formation classes, mental prayer, spiritual reading, etc. How many respond? The excuses are as varied as the excuses given to the bridegroom in the Gospel parable who had provided the wedding feast: jobs, leisure, entertainment, sports, vacations and various other appointments today command more of our attention than time for God. Yet, if we give up a tennis match to attend a day of recollection or a leisurely weekend for a retreat, we are paid in dividends greater than any earthly treasure.

Another common misunderstanding about sanctity is that it is extraordinary. Sometimes we tend to think that only those who have visions, apparitions, locutions, or who work miracles are capable of becoming saints. Although the grace of God is miraculous and supernatural, it is normally granted to us through the ordinary means of God's providence. Remember the Little Flower: she won her sanctity through the "little things" of each day, just as our sanctity is won by raising each of our actions to God during the day. Every day thousands of lay people around the world are striving to become saints by sanctifying themselves through their ordinary work.

Along with cooperating with the grace of God, we have to fulfill all God's commands, for He said, *"If you keep my commandments you will abide in my love"* (Jn. 15:10).

Remember how Jesus called the Pharisees hypocrites because they conformed to the letter of the law, but not to the spirit? Likewise, Christ's law does not involve the mere fulfillment of external practices, but rather requires an internal identification with the mind and heart of Jesus. Only through this identification with Christ can we fully cooperate with the sanctifying power of divine grace.

For example, a person can go to Mass and Holy Communion on Sunday, listen to the Gospel and the homily, then rush out of Mass early, dent a fender in the parking lot but neglect to leave his name and phone number, argue with his wife, drink too much that evening and, at work on Monday, neglect his responsibilities while undermining another's work out of envy. He is only conforming to the letter of Christ's law by fulfilling his obligation to attend Mass on Sunday. If he were conforming to the spirit of the law, he would make a prayerful thanksgiving after Communion. After leaving Church, if he dented a car fender pulling out of the parking space, he would leave his name and telephone number so that he could pay restitution to the owner of the car. When tension mounts at home, he would cooperate with actual grace by controlling his temper, rather than arguing with his wife. By moderating his intake of alcohol, he would be exercising the virtue of temperance. Monday at work despite the stressful Sunday, he would again cooperate with God's graces and put in a full day's work for a full day's pay. He would be able to battle and win the struggle with envy over his associates' successes. All this would be possible because of grace and his cooperation with grace. He would be conforming to the *spirit* of the law.

A Christian who is destined for heaven can only find peace, joy, happiness and contentment when he or she cooperates with the gift of grace. If we are only satisfied with the fulfillment of the natural law precepts (the Ten Commandments) but neglect the sacraments by which we can grow in grace, we lose great opportunities which God is giving us for spiritual growth. That is why we have so many people still searching for their identities while in their 30s, 40s and even older.

Through the choices that we make during each day, we determine the direction of our entire lives. None of our patterns are necessarily immutable: one day we choose good and the next we may choose evil. At one moment we seek God and, in almost the same sentence, we seek the love of self. A good person can sin and a sinner can be converted. For this reason we have to be continually watchful and exert effort to maintain our determination to seek God, the *only* perfect Good.

Virtue and Us

In order to keep our wills permanently going in the right direction, we have to acquire certain habits that we have been discussing called acquired moral *virtues*. Every single human act inclines the will more firmly toward the object of the act, and the repetition of acts of the same kind builds up habits. We build up physical or mechanical habits in a similar manner. By typing frequently, we become faster and make fewer errors. Each time we play tennis we get a bit faster, a little sharper, and our game improves. It is the same with bad habits. Each time we tell a "little white lie" to get us out of a tight corner, we develop the habit of lying. The same happens with other moral habits: being fair in our judgment of others or being critical; being courageous in the face of danger or being a coward; being reflective or being impulsive. These moral habits are the result of exercise or repetition of single acts of the same kind. If the acts are good, the result is a good habit or *virtue*. If the acts are bad, the result is a bad habit or *vice*. Both virtues and vices incline the will more firmly toward a particular object: a good object in the case of virtue, or an evil object in the case of vice.

Virtues play a crucial role in our moral life, as they give our will a certain direction toward what is good. We are not good when we do good only occasionally. We are only good when we do good habitually, even when "we don't feel like it." An irascible person who is patient once in a while remains irascible and does not become a patient person just by an occasional act of patience. That person must struggle daily with every situation until patience becomes a habit. The same is true for the person who is a chronic complainer. Each time the person complains, the vice gets a bit more imbedded in his or her will and character. Each time the person stifles a complaint, virtue *begins* to grow.

Good habits, virtues, give a person a certain kinship with those particular goods. Thus the person who practices justice acquires the habit of giving to each person his due, the particular good that justice attains; he becomes a just person and more attuned to the demands of justice. The more virtues a person has, the more firmly he is inclined toward different moral goods. He raises the atmosphere around him, bringing peace, happiness, cheerfulness, contentment. His actions improve society and the world at large. Nonetheless, this does not mean to say that a virtuous person can no longer do evil. Even a virtuous person has the freedom to use his free will incorrectly and turn toward an evil object.

Let's consider for a moment how we acquire virtues. For our example we will take a person who has the bad habit of overeating. He decides to develop the virtue of temperance. He plans to say "no" to all second helpings. At home, although still hungry, he passes up seconds and skips snacks. Lunching at a buffet, he only goes around once and is moderate in taking the various foods. Cooking for himself, he makes only a moderate portion. By these constant acts of temperance he will eventually become temperate in his eating habits, but it takes time, will power and constantly saying "no" to himself before this is achieved. If he is not vigilant, he may find himself practicing temperance only part of the time. At home he may be careful; but when at a buffet, because he is paying for it, he feels compelled to overeat. By falling for this line of reasoning, he slips back into the sin of gluttony.

As we struggle to acquire a particular virtue, practice makes it come more easily, more spontaneously. A woman who lacks the virtue of cheerfulness may struggle to put a smile on her face every time she meets someone she knows. When this becomes natural, she may begin struggling to smile at strangers. When this becomes a habit, she will struggle to be cheerful in the face of sorrows and disappointments. Eventually this woman will be known as a cheerful person.

Not every habit is a virtue. It can be a meaningless act such as thumb-sucking or a vice such as stealing. Virtues are "only those actions which improve or perfect an action and move us toward the good."[8] Virtues help our will to act easily and naturally in the most perfect manner.

[8] John A. Hardon, SJ, *The Catholic Catechism* (Garden City, New York: Doubleday & Company, Inc., 1975), p. 196.

An indifferent habit can help us to develop a virtue. Some little girls have the habit of twisting their hair around a finger. The little girl who is trying to break the habit may be cultivating the virtue of self-control each time she resists the impulse to play with her hair.

While we may be working to cultivate one virtue, others naturally come into play. The person who is struggling to develop humility may also grow in self-control when he avoids boasting, bragging or putting himself first. St. Thomas Aquinas says that we grow in the various virtues like a hand grows. Each finger is separate but joined to the hand. The virtues develop, interweave and overlap.

It is important to realize that the *acquired* moral virtues may exist in a person who is not in the state of grace. But the acquired moral virtues in a person in mortal sin are somewhat unstable; they are not yet in the state of solid virtue. This is because a man or woman in mortal sin is habitually turned away from God. Instead of loving Him above all else, the person loves himself or herself more than God. As a result, there is a weakness or a partial lack of ability to accomplish moral good, even of the natural order. The acquired virtues in such a person lack solidity because they are not connected, not supported by the closely related infused moral virtues.

Virtues Come In Several Varieties

Virtues are of various types. We have been discussing acquired moral virtues. On just the natural level people struggle daily to acquire virtues so that they can become more competent and competitive in their fields. No one can advance very far in his profession or field until he or she learns to acquire the virtues of *order, obedience, perseverance, self-control, industriousness* and *responsibility.* An athlete struggles to acquire the virtues of *courage, daring, fortitude, audacity* and *optimism.* Parents work to acquire the virtues of *patience, flexibility, understanding, loyalty* and *generosity* with and toward their children. People on diets battle to acquire the virtues of *temperance, moderation* and *prudence* in regard to food. So it goes. These virtues can be acquired by Christians and non-Christians. They help us to improve on a purely natural level. Through them we become more successful in the eyes of the world, win races, become thinner and less self-centered. If our reason for acquiring these virtues is purely personal gain or worldly concerns, they are simply acquired virtues, similar to the virtues practiced by the Greeks and the ancient Romans.

On the highest level are the *infused theological virtues* of faith, hope, and charity given by God with the "infusion" of sanctifying grace along with the four infused virtues of prudence, justice, temperance and fortitude, which direct us (or incline us) to pursue the moral good for the sake of our supernatural goal. Without them, we would sink to the pursuit of temporal goods. The infused virtues enable us to perform acts that are worthy of children of God and are, therefore, meritorious. To put it more precisely, the infused virtues are perfections enabling the intellect and the will to function beyond their natural range.

Our natural or human virtues are also perfected by sanctifying grace. To better understand this, consider this example: a person who is well organized and a hard worker, who exercises good judgment and is fair with his fellow men, may not yet know all there is to know about running a business with efficiency. However, once he has acquired this knowledge, which is also a new quality, he brings all his former qualities into the efficient management of his business. In a similar manner, by the new divine quality of sanctifying grace, all the acquired moral virtues receive a new perfection. "God causes this increase when we receive the sacraments, perform good works, or recite our prayers."[9] When we receive the sacraments, depending on our dispositions, we receive varying increases of sanctifying grace and the infused virtues. Again the increase depends on our dispositions. Our prayer also obtains an increase of grace and of virtue in proportion to the fervor with which we pray.[10] This is how the infused virtues take deeper root within our souls.

Frequent and deliberate venial sin "does hinder considerably the exercise of these virtues, by lessening the facility ac-

---

[9] *The Spiritual Life—A Treatise On Ascetical And Mystical Theology*, *op. cit.*, p. 475, n.1005B.
[10] *Ibid.*, p.474, n.1003A.

quired through previous acts. This facility is the result of earnestness and perseverance in effort; but deliberate venial faults chill our ardor, and partly paralyze our activity....Venial sins against the virtue of temperance, though they do not detract from that infused virtue itself, gradually lessen the facility once acquired for mortifying sensuality. Besides, abuse of grace causes a reduction of the number of actual graces that help in the exercise of the virtues, and on this account the practice of virtue lacks vigor. Lastly, we have stated, deliberate venial faults pave the way for grave ones and thereby for the loss of the virtues."[11]

Consider the example of a renowned violinist. The violinist is gifted with a tremendous natural musical ability. His fingers fly over the strings effortlessly because of his years of practice (acquired virtues). If he loses the use of his hands, he can no longer play the violin. His mind is still keen but his fingers no longer obey his brilliant mind. He is no longer a violinist. God's grace in regard to the infused moral virtues sharpens us supernaturally to become more perfect. It encourages us to strive for sanctity but we cannot fly spiritually until we acquire the natural virtues ourselves.

How Are You Responding to God's Call?

God makes sanctification so accessible to us. He gives us the ability and the necessary tools to become saints. All we can do, and are asked to do, is to cooperate with the sanctifying power of God's grace. Without grace, no one can be saved or sanctified. That is why the Sacrament of Reconciliation is so important. It's up to us to cooperate with all His generous gifts.[12]

As we continue our spiritual journey, let's consider the words of Monsignor Escrivá: "To live according to the Holy Spirit means to live by faith and hope and charity—to allow God to take possession of our lives and to change our hearts, to

---

[11] *Ibid.*, p. 475, n.1004A.
[12] Portions of this chapter were taken from Chapters 2 & 12 of the book, *You Can Become A Saint!* by Mary Ann Budnik (Houston: Lumen Christi Press, 1990).

make us resemble Him more...This is how the early Christians lived, and this is how we too should live: meditating the doctrine of our faith until it becomes a part of us; receiving our Lord in the Eucharist; meeting Him in the personal dialogue of our prayer, without trying to hide behind an impersonal conduct, but face to face with Him. These means should become the very substance of our attitude. If we are lacking we will have, perhaps, the ability to think in an erudite manner, an activity that is more or less intense, some practices and devotions. *But we will not have an authentically Christian way of life, because we are all equally called to sanctity. There are no second-class Christians obliged to practice only a 'simplified version' of the Gospel.*"[13]

In summary, the goal of our life is to live as God's daughters and sons, to be the person God wants us to be. But we are all weak; we are prone to sin, and we fall many times. We can work against God's virtues and commandments, and turn away from the gifts He has given us. We need to examine our consciences well on a daily basis and go to confession frequently.

If you are looking for peace, try confession! The Sacrament of Reconciliation is not something to fear nor dread. It's actually the gateway through which we obtain peace, holiness, and happiness in this world, and eternity with God in the next. What a wonderful gift from such a loving God! Use it well.

[13] Monsignor Josemaría Escrivá de Balaguer, *Christ is Passing By* (Chicago: Scepter, 1974), n.134.

Appendix A

Examination Of Conscience—
How Am I Doing?

An examination of conscience can be frightful or over-whelming. Or it can be a mere "piece of cake." In reality, it probably should be somewhere in the middle. We are all sin-ners, so if we can get through a complete examination of con-science in just a couple of minutes, or recap a whole week's worth of mishaps in only a heartbeat, then either we have missed a whole lot of evils, or we aren't serious about what we are doing...or probably both.

On the other hand, most of us don't need to go through pages of evil deeds or spend hours trying to determine if we fit in somehow with every sin committed in our part of the world in the last so many days or weeks.

So if we are somewhere in the middle, what does that really mean? Well, it probably means we tend to forget some sins we shouldn't forget, and tend to be overly critical about some sins while under-estimating others.

So, in other words, we just need a good summary to run through. And that is what follows...an over-done list of many, many sins in the anticipation that you will be able to better identify with the ones that you need to bring to Jesus in the per-son of the priest and the use of the Sacrament of Reconciliation.

143

(Feel free to add any I might have missed.)

1. Did I fail to love God...to pray? Do I put God first in my life? Do I have the right intention in all my actions? Did I omit morning or evening prayers? Was I careless or distracted in saying my prayers? Have I doubted or denied my Faith? Read books against the Catholic Faith? Was I guilty of idolatry, irreligion, tempting God, sacrilege, or simony? Did I give in to despair, presumption, spiritual sloth? Do I accept *all* the teachings of the Catholic Church? Do I fearlessly profess my faith? Am I a Christian in my private and public life? Did I seriously doubt my faith? Was I guilty of promoting heresy, deliberate doubt, or religious indifferentism? Did I engage in palm-reading, fortunetelling, psychics, tarot cards? Did I get involved in the occult or in non-Catholic sects? Did I receive Communion in the state of mortal sin? Did I intentionally fail to confess some mortal sin in my previous confession? Do I support the Church, my parish, other worthwhile causes? Did I keep the required fasts and abstinences? Am I proud, boastful? Do I despise others?

2. Did I curse, swear or, make a false oath? Did I use God or the name of Jesus in vain: lightly...carelessly...by blasphemy? Did I use profane language? Have I insulted a sacred person? Was I disrespectful toward the Blessed Virgin or the saints? Did I break any vows that I have made?

3. Have I missed Mass through my own fault? On Sundays? Holy Days? Was I late for Mass or did I leave early without a good reason? Allow my children to miss Mass? Did I omit my Easter Duty? Or my yearly confession duty? Was I easily distracted at Mass? Do unnecessary work on Sunday? Needlessly shop on Sunday? In a positive sense did I use Sunday for spiritual, family, and cultural activities?

4. Did I honor and obey my parents? Have I been disrespectful, unkind, or neglectful toward my parents? Have I been helpful to them in spiritual and material needs? Have I talked back to my parents? Failed to help at

home?   Been sad or sour? Do I neglect my children's
religious education?   Failed to lead them to   Holy
Mass. . .to frequent confession?   Failed to spend time
with my family? Have I cared for the material and
spiritual needs of my children? Have I been patient with
my spouse and children? Do I show good example to
family members? Have I exercised authority as a parent?
Do I obey lawful authority?

5.   Was I angry. . .resentful. . .kept hatred in my heart?
Drunk or on drugs? Did I fight. . .give bad example or
scandal? Did I fail to correct in charity? Permitted or
encouraged an abortion or mutilation (vasectomy, sterilization, etc.) to avoid children? Did I take part in mercy
killing, genocide, rioting, an unjust war, or physical and
verbal abuse? Do I profess to be opposed to abortion but
promote abortion legislation or pro-abortion candidates,
regulations, forced population control? Do I work to
overturn immoral government legislation such as abortion, mercy killing, etc.? Do I refuse to forgive? Did I
hurt or try to kill anyone? Am I a glutton? Did I give bad
example or scandal? Did I damage anything in anger?
Have I made reparation to others for my harmful words,
actions, or bad example?   Was I guilty of discord,
quarrels, angry words, antagonism, tantrums, the "silent
treatment," selfishness, pride, pettiness, insults, bossiness, or being inconsiderate? Do I use people for my
own ends? Am I estranged from others through quarrels
or insults? Am I selfish? If injured, have I forgiven the
person/persons involved?   Do I care for my health
adequately? Am I obsessed with my weight to the point
of endangering my health? Am I patient in the face of
suffering, disappointments, and sorrows?

6.   Did I consent to impure glances? Passionate kisses such
as French kissing? Sinful touches such as petting, necking, etc.? Was I immodest in dress, behavior? Did I read
pornographic books, or magazines? Did I produce, sell or

give pornographic material to others? Do I willfully look at indecent pictures or watch immoral movies? Did I engage in impure jokes or conversations? Did I willfully entertain impure thoughts or feelings? Am I guilty of masturbation (impurity with self), fornication (premarital sex), adultery (sex with married person) or birth control (by pills, devices, withdrawal)? Did I engage in incest, rape, or homosexual acts? Have I caused others to sin by my example? Do I avoid laziness, idleness, and the occasions of impurity? Have I been faithful to my spouse in my heart and relations with others? Do I watch soap operas or TV interview shows that promote immorality? Do I engage in undue familiarity with the opposite sex? Do I guard my eyes?

7.   Did I steal, rob, accept bribes, shoplift, vandalize, or commit fraud? Did I copy printed materials, audio and video tapes without permission? Am I guilt of employee theft by taking supplies, objects, wasting time or making personal long distance phone calls? Have I involved others in a loss? What or how much? Did I return it or make equal restitution? Have I been honest in all my business relations? Have I dealt honestly with insurance companies? Cheat my employer or customers? Do I pay a fair wage to my employees? Do I charge exorbitant fees for my services? Am I guilty of usury (charging excessive interest rates)? As an employee am I guilty of absenteeism or non- cooperation thereby injuring the industry I work for? Have I been honest in workman's compensation claims? Am I faithful to my promises and contracts? Am I honest and hard-working, serving others? As a politician, economist, or trade union leader do I work diligently, morally, and wisely for the public I represent? Do I support evil or exploit it? Am I in a position to avoid, eliminate, or limit certain social evils but fail to do so out of laziness, fear, indifference, payoffs, or the conspiracy of silence? Did I damage another's property? Did I waste time in school, at home? Do I cheat on tests? Am I stingy? Do I gamble or shop excessively? Am I excessively involved in sports or hobbies? Neglect to pay my debts

promptly? Do I live poverty of spirit and detachment?
Do I share my possessions and money with the poor,
oppressed, or misfortunate? Have I paid my taxes and
exercised good citizenship? Do I tend to be lazy? Am I
prone to avarice, miserliness, niggardliness, or luxury
where I must have the latest and the best?

8.   Have I lied, criticized, gossiped, or revealed secrets?
Talked about another behind his or her back? Have I destroyed someone's good name? Am I guilty of libel,
slander, detraction, or calumny? Did I sin in regard to
flattery or speaking excessively? Did I judge rashly?
How many persons listened to my derogatory remarks?
Do I always tell the truth? Am I sincere? Do I spread
rumors or false information? Am I critical, negative, or
uncharitable in my talk? Do I look down on the poor,
sick, elderly, strangers, lower classes, or people of other
races? Did I go against my conscience out of hypocrisy
or fear? Do I give in to morbid curiosity, backbiting,
ridiculing, unfairness, injustice, persecution, or discord?
Have I tried to make reparation for the harm I have
caused by my words?

9.   Have I consented to impure thoughts? Have I caused
them by stares, bad reading, curiosity, or impure conversations? Do I neglect to control my imagination? Do
I pray at once to banish bad thoughts and temptations?
Am I living in adultery? Did I obey the laws of the
Church in regard to marriage or remarriage? Am I mod-
est and chaste in my clothing and manner of acting?

10.   Is my heart greedy? Am I envious of what another
has? Am I jealous of someone? Am I moody? Gloomy?
Do I work, study and keep busy to counter idle
thoughts? Is my heart set on earthly possessions or on
the true treasures in heaven? Am I consumed by acquiring more possessions, money, or power? Do I boast or
am I vain? Am I consumed by ambition to the detriment
of family life and my spiritual growth? Do I sin in regard to ostentation and hypocrisy?

Appendix B

Examination Of Conscience—
Ages 7-10 Years Old

- Do I say my morning and night prayers with real purpose, and do I try to think of God at different times through the day? Do I pay attention at Mass, especially at the Consecration, thinking of what's happening?

- Have I saddened my parents, teachers, etc. by my behavior? Am I disobedient to them?

- Do I know and accept the fact that my "job" right now consists of school work and my tasks at home? Do I look for ways to get out of these jobs, or do I do them poorly?

- Do I give bad example to my brothers, sisters or friends in my attitude or actions?

- Do I get carried away by bad moods and get angry often without real reason?

- Do I have the bad habit of always thinking of myself first? For example, am I unhappy unless I win a game, am first in line, get all the food I like, get to go where I want to go, etc.?

- Am I selfish about my things? Does it bother me to have to share them with my brothers and sisters?

- When I am sick or hurt, do I try not to complain? Do I try to offer up times when I hurt as a private sacrifice to God?

- Do I try to help my friends and family when they need it? Do I wait to be asked to help, or do I look for ways to do so on my own?

- Do I realize how important it is to tell the truth and to be sincere at home, at school and in talking to God in prayer?

APPENDIX C

Examination Of Conscience—
Ages 11-16 Years Old

- Do I say my morning and night prayers with real purpose, and do I try to think of God at different times of the day?

- Have I missed Mass on Sundays or Holy Days by making no real effort of my own to get to Church? Was I voluntarily distracted at Mass? Did I talk to friends during Mass? Did I get to Mass late and/or leave early? Did I participate in the Mass? Do I donate a portion of my allowance to the offertory collection?

- Have I spoken irreverently about holy things, the Sacraments, the Church or its ministers? Have I uttered the name of God or Jesus in disrespectful ways in my conversation with friends? Do I curse or swear?

- Do I have an excessive desire for independence which causes me to receive badly the commands of my parents and teachers? Do I realize that this reactions stems from pride?

- Have I quarreled too much with my brothers, sisters, friends, parents?

- Am I aware that I have a principal fault? Am I struggling to identify and get rid of this fault?

- Do I try to control my appetite for material things (food, clothes, possessions, entertainment)? Do I get angry if things don't work out as I plan or want? Do I respect authority and try to learn from disappointments rather than letting them get the best of me?

- Do I study hard and with order, realizing that by doing so I make best use of the talents God has given me, and show appreciation for the effort my parents make to educate me?

- Do I treat my peers with respect and am I aware of the needs of others around me? Do I respect the possessions and property of other people?

- Have I given in to dishonesty, especially by lying, cheating or stealing, either to avoid getting into trouble or for my personal benefit?

- Do I take drugs, drink, get drunk?

- Do I observe the details of modesty which safeguard purity? Have I seen bad movies, TV shows, videos? Have I read immoral magazines, books or other material? Have I allowed my companions to convince me to participate in any of these activities? Have I allowed myself to be carried away by desires opposed to the virtue of purity? Do I dress modesty? Do I avoid situations that could lead to sins against the virtue of chastity with myself, with others?

- Have I really worked on my personal relationship with God, asking for special graces in times of temptation or important discussions?

Appendix D

Examination Of Conscience—
For Teenagers and Young Adults

- Did I often think about my Father, God, today as I went about my work and sports at home and at school?

- Did I try to be aware of my Brother, Jesus, in the nearest Tabernacle, and even pay Him a visit if it was possible?

- Did I call upon the Holy Spirit for guidance in difficult or unusual situations?

- Did I sometimes glance at pictures of my Mother, Mary, say something loving to her in my heart, and ask for her help in my needs?

- Did I remember to thank God for everything— especially for my health and talents, for my home and parents, and for the country and the world in which I live?

- Did I also think about my Guardian Angel and thank him for his constant protection?

- Do I ask God to let me see how He wants me to spend my life; what He wants my vocation to be?

- In my relations with friends and with other members of the family did I try to help them in some way, instead of always looking out for my own enjoyment or comfort?

- Did I make things more difficult for others because of my lack of cooperation or stubbornness?

- In particular, did I resist requests or advice from my elders, or talk back to them?

- Was I too much attached to my own things when someone else wanted to use or borrow them?

- Is there a general lack of generosity in my conduct which needs to be corrected?

- Did I use money responsibly, or did I spend it unwisely or selfishly— even if it was only a small amount?

- Do I participate in the family rosary, say grace before meals, morning and night prayers?

- Do I remember to pray for the Holy Father and for all the Bishops who help him govern the Church?

- Do I also pray for those who are responsible for the well-being of our country and of the locality where I live?

- When I am puzzled or confused about some point of Catholic faith or morals, do I talk it over with one of my parents?

- What am I doing to prepare my soul for my next Communion so that it will be more beneficial than ever before?

- Has it been too long since my last confession?

- If I am aware of a serious offense against God or another person or myself, when is the soonest I can confess it to the priest and receive God's pardon, along with the grace I need to struggle against my faults?

Examination of Conscience—
For Teenagers and Young Adults

- Did I complain about things too much— especially if there was nothing anyone could do about the situation?

- Did I offer to God my pains, discomforts, and disappointments in atonement for my own faults and those of others?

- Do I also remember to make small sacrifices for the people in the world who are suffering persecution and for those who are offending God?

- Did I spend enough time studying, or did I neglect it for poor reasons?

- Am I trying to carry out my tasks quickly and do them better than yesterday— without having to be reminded?

- Did I spend too much time "fooling around" instead of helping out at home or trying to improve my school work?

- Specifically, did I waste time on excessive television, games, tapes, phone conversations, or day dreaming?

- Did I try to guard my eyes and ears, avoiding looking at or listening to anything immodest, indecent, or otherwise degrading. Have I committed any impure acts alone or with another such as masturbation, homosexual acts, pre-marital sex?

- Did I have an abortion or help a friend to procure one?

- Do I always try to avoid anything that would offend God, harm others, or damage my own life and reputation such as taking drugs, drinking to get drunk, contemplating suicide?

- If any bad thoughts came into my mind today did I try to "switch the channel" in my mind to something good right away?

- Was I careful to dress and act modestly so as not to give bad thoughts to others?

- Do I try to take good care of my clothes, possessions, and other things at home and at school/work in order to make them last longer? Am I an honest employee?

- Did I respect my parents and strive to treat them well— even if there was a disagreement? Do I realize that God has given me into their care and that I should pray for them and for their needs?

- Did I try to see my own faults and not just those of others?

- Do I ask God for help in overcoming my own faults?

- Was there any lack of truthfulness in my speech or conversation at home, school, or work? If so, how can I make up for it and prevent it from happening again?

- Did I give in to anger and say or do things which I now regret? If so, how can I make up for it tomorrow?

- Did I start a fight, intentionally irritate someone, or in any way contribute to an ugly scene?

- Was I guilty of bad example in my speech or conduct with my friends? If so, what caused it, and how can I make up for it?

- In my relations with my best friend, do I avoid anything embarrassing or excessively intimate?

- Do I always try to be cheerful, especially when I don't feel well or something has gone wrong?

- Was I jealous or envious of the good fortune of others?

Examination Of Conscience—
For Parents

- Am I always striving to be more generous with God in my personal life, recognizing the undeserved generosity He has had with me and with the family?

- Do I constantly give the example of love and respect for the Church and the Holy Father, and for all priests and religious, showing the children how to cover over the personal failings of a priest or nun?

- Am I constantly vigilant to take advantage of the most propitious moments to remind each child of his responsibility to God and to the Church as well as to other people?

- Do I, in particular, look for the most effective way to nourish in each child the practice of frequent confession, taking care that they understand the reason for it?

- Do the furnishings of our home contain the traditional reminders of God's presence (a crucifix, tasteful pictures or small statues of Our Lord and His Mother, etc.), without going to the extreme of converting the home into a convent?

- Do I make sure that traditional family prayers such as the rosary, grace before meals, morning and evening prayers are not lost in the rush of activities as the family grows and becomes involved with sports, etc.?

- Do I try to familiarize myself with the content and the tone of the religious instruction and sex education my children are receiving through the parish or school, realizing that as a parent I have the primary responsibility to see that they receive a correct and complete knowledge of Catholic doctrine and morals?

- Do I encourage questions about faith and morals so as to clarify problems when they first arise and before they turn into doubt and disbelief?

- Do I help them to develop the crucial virtue of sincerity especially in these matters of faith and morals?

- Do I try to be absolutely fair in my treatment of all the children, showing no favoritism for one in particular?

- Do I try to cultivate the good will and love of each child, trying to be a real friend and confidant?

- Do I moderate my zeal to protect the children from experience with the inevitable imperfection of life in this world, teaching them to turn those experiences to good effect?

- Do I show the children— by word and example— that the only thing to be ashamed of is sin— offending God?

- Do I try to respect the independent judgment of the children (especially the older ones), realizing that it is necessary for them to learn from their own mistakes, as I did when I was their age?

- If is was necessary to correct one of the children did I first consult my spouse, wait until my anger had subsided, and then make the correction in private?

- Did I refrain from corporal punishment or other sanctions unless it was absolutely necessary?

- Do I try to make sure that each child is always fully occupied with constructive work, study, or wholesome recreation, always thinking ahead for suggestions to fill unexpected idle moments?

- Am I constantly vigilant about what the children see on television, videos, movies, read in books, magazines, and newspapers that come into the house— quietly and undramatically exercising any necessary censorship?

- Do I exercise constant but quiet attention to the particular friendships of my children, seeking to know who their companions are, what they are like, and what they do together?

- Do I try to inculcate respect for money, cars, possessions, and care for material things around the home as the children grow?

YOU CAN BECOME A SAINT!

BY
MARY ANN BUDNIK

YOU ARE CALLED TO BE A SAINT!

Sainthood isn't optional. Pope John Paul II told us New Orleans (1987): "The world needs...saints.Holiness is not the privilege of a few; it is a gift offered to all."

BUT AREN'T SAINTS SPECIAL PEOPLE?

No! Saints are people like you and like me. Saints become saints by the way they live their lives. With the grace of God, our determination, and applying what the experts consider the A B C's of becoming a saint, we can all grow in holiness. First published in 1990, this second printing is in response to public demand.

WHAT TOPICS ARE COVERED?

Topics covered include the universal call to sanctity; graces and how they effect our souls; the theological, moral and natural virtues and how we can obtain them; a plan for growing in holiness; sanctifying our daily work; order; the role of angels in our lives; mental prayer; what to read to grow in holiness; the problem of sin, the commandments, and the sacrament of penance; the power of Holy Mass and the Blessed Sacrament and why we need them; how to develop devotion to Our Lady and her rosary; why suffer?; how to perseverance in striving for holiness; and fascinating examples from the lives of the saints.

WHAT ARE PEOPLE SAYING ABOUT THE BOOK?

"You Can Become A Saint! is a treasure of spiritual and practical wisdom for the Catholic laity. Page after page is filled with down-to-earth directives on how to become holy in today's secularized world...This book makes fascinating reading. But far more important, it tells the believing Christian how to be holy and happy here on earth, in anticipation of that blessed eternity for which we were made." **John A. Hardon, S.J., Author, Theologian, and Consultant for the Holy See and the *Catechism of the Catholic Church*.**

YOU CAN BECOME A SAINT! is $13.95 and can be purchased from your local Catholic Bookstore or R.B. Media, Inc.

Bibliography

Alberione, Rev. James SSP, STD. *Daily Meditations*. Boston, 1983.

Amorth, Fr. Gabrielle. *Inside the Vatican*. Rome, 1994.

A Primer for the Catechism of the Catholic Church. Rome, 1994.

Augustine, St. *Daily Readings with St. Augustine*. Springfield, 1986. *The Confessions of St. Augustine*. New York, 1943

Budnik, Mary Ann. *You Can Become A Saint!* Houston, 1990.

Bossis, Gabrielle. *He and I* Quebec, 1969.

Catechism of the Catholic Church. Boston, 1994.

Companion to the Catechism of the Catholic Church. San Francisco, 1994.

Council of Trent Documents.

Cristiani, Msgr. Leon. *The Story of Monica and Her Son Augustine*. Boston, 1977.

Caraman, Philip, S.J. *Saints and Ourselves*. New York, 1953.

D'Ars, Cure. *Thoughts of the Cure D'Ars*. Rockford, 1984.

Daughters of St. Paul. *Basic Catechism*. Boston, 1984.

Doherty, Eddie. *Matt Talbot*. Milwaukee, 1953.

Dubay, Thomas SM. *Seeking Spiritual Direction*. Ann Arbor, 1993.

Escrivá de Balaguer, Blessed Josemaría. *Christ is Passing By*. New York, 1980. *The Forge*. New York, 1988 *Furrow*. New York, 1987. *The Way*. New York, 1954.

Hardon, John A., SJ. *The Question and Answer Catholic Catechism*. New York, 1981. *Spiritual Life in the Modern World*. Boston, 1982. *The Catholic Catechism*. New York, 1975.

Herbst, Winfrid, S.D.S. *Follow the Saints*. New York, 1933.

Hickey, James Cardinal. *Mary at the Foot of the Cross*. San Francisco, 1989.

Huber, George, *My Angel Will Go Before You*. Dublin, 1983.

Hughes, Philip. *The Faith in Practice*. New York, 1937.

Knox, Ronald. *The Layman and His Conscience*. New York, 1961.

Kowalska, Blessed Faustina. *Divine Mercy in My Soul*. Stockbridge, 1987.

Louis of Granada, Venerable. *The Sinner's Guide*. Rockford, 1883.

Luna, Rev. F. *Making the Most of Confession*. New York, 1982.

McArdle, Jack. "Holiness," *The Voice Of Padre Pio* Magazine. Italy Vol. XVIII, #4, 1988.

Malaise, Joseph SJ. *Know Yourself*. (Audio tapes) Springfield, 1992.

McElhone, James F., CSC. *Particular Examen—How to Root Out Hidden Faults*. Harrison, 1952.

McHugh, John A. O.P., Callan, Charles J. , O.P., revised by Farrell, Edward P., O.P. *Moral Theology*. New York, 1958.

Menendez, Sister Josefa. *I Wait for You*—Sections from *The Way of Divine Love*. Rockford, 1985.

More, Thomas. *The Sadness of Christ*. Princeton, 1993.

Petrisko, Thomas W. *Call of the Ages*. Santa Barbara, 1995.

Pontifical Council for the Family. *The Truth and Meaning of Human Sexuality*. Rome, 1996.

Pope John Paul II, *The Gospel of Life*. 1995. *On the Holy Spirit in the Life of the Church and the World*. 1986. Press Release from San Antonio, TX, 1987. *Reconciliation and Penance*. 1984. *Tertio Millennio Adveniente*. 1994. *The Splendor of Truth*. 1993. *The Role of the Christian Family in the Modern World*. 1981. *Catechesi Tradendae (On Catechesis in our Time)*. 1979.

Pope Paul VI. *Indulgeniarm Doctrina* (Apostolic Constitution on the Revision of Indulgences). 1967. *Declaration on Christian Education*. 1965.

Pope Pius XI. *On Christian Marriage*. 1930.

O'Sullivan, Paul, O.P. *The Secret of Confession*. Rockford, 1936.

Our Lady Queen of Peace. Newspaper. Spring, 1995.

Rego, Father Richard J. *Guide to Conscience*. St. Paul, 1990.

Rite of Penance. Washington, DC, 1975

Sheen, Fulton J. *Lift Up Your Heart*. Garden City, 1952. *Peace of Soul*. Garden City, 1951. *These Are the Sacraments*. New York, 1962.

Illinois State-Journal Register. "Survey On Confession Shows Different Views." Springfield, March 11, 1990.

Sacred Congregation for Catholic Education. *Education Guidance in Human Love* (Outlines for Sex Education). 1983.

Sacred Congregation for the Doctrine of the Faith. *Declaration on Certain Questions Concerning Sexual Ethics*. 1975.

Suarez, Frederico, *Penance*. New Rochelle, 1987.

Tanquerey, Adolphe, SS, DD. *The Spiritual Life—A Treastise on Ascetical and Mystical Theology*. Belgium, 1930.

Trese, Leo J. *The Faith Explained*. Chicago, 1959.

Torello, Msgr. G. B. "Apologia For A Piece Of Church Furniture." *Homiletic & Pastoral Review*. Feb., 1994.

Vaughan, Bishop John S. *Venial Sin*. London, 1923.

Vatican II Documents. *Lumen Gentium*.

Wall Street Journal. "White Fright." New York, 1995.

Wilson, Alfred, CP. *Pardon and Peace*, New York, 1965.

Index

A

Abortion: 10, 38, 40, 47, 59, 60,
  65, 68, 77, 78, 85, 86, 90, 91,
  95, 96, 98
Absolution: 21, 25, 29, 103, 121,
  122
Act of Contrition: 120
Adam: 7, 8, 9, 25
Adultery: 18, 25, 46, 70, 79, 80, 99
Ambition: 2, 3, 41, 42, 43, 44
Amendment: 108, 110
Apostasy: 56, 72
Archbishop Fulton Sheen (Fulton
  Sheen): 3, 21, 22, 97
Atheism: 56, 72

B

Baptism: 14, 25, 26, 28, 29, 74,
  125, 131
Blasphemy (blasphemies): 58,
  61, 74
Blessed Faustina: 30, 57, 91, 103
Blessed Josemaría Escrivá de
  Balaguer: 124
Blessed Matt Talbot: 20
Boasting: 41, 42, 63, 139

C

Capital punishment: 79
Chastity: 19, 40, 80, 83, 94, 107,
  108, 118
Church: 5, 12, 18, 19, 20, 21, 25,
  26, 27, 28, 29, 31, 32, 33, 35,
  37, 38, 39, 40, 44, 52, 56, 61,
  65, 67, 68, 69, 70, 72, 73, 74,
  75, 76, 77, 83, 84, 86, 95,
  100, 101, 105, 109, 110, 113,
  117, 118, 120, 122, 123, 125,
  128, 132, 134, 136
Concupiscence of the eyes: 62, 63
Concupiscence of the flesh: 62
Conscience: 11, 23, 27, 29, 32,
  33, 45, 49, 51, 52, 57, 60, 67,
  93, 95, 96, 97, 98, 99, 100,
  101, 103, 104, 105, 106, 107,
  108, 113, 115, 121, 122, 142
Contraception:
  32, 35, 46, 59, 96
Contrition (perfect & imperfect):
  109, 110, 120
Conversion: 11, 12, 16, 17, 19,
  28, 34, 35, 36, 73, 88, 94,
  107, 109, 113, 121
Courage: 2, 13, 15, 17, 20, 23,
  28, 31, 32, 33, 53, 77, 85,
  105, 125, 134, 137, 139
Cross: 5, 6, 14, 16, 20, 23,
  32, 51, 91, 105, 113, 119
Crucifixion: 17, 26
Cure of Ars (St. John Vianney): 101
Curses: 58

D

Death: 1, 7, 8, 11, 14, 16, 18, 20,
  23, 30, 32, 33, 36, 43, 51, 55,
  56, 60, 78, 96, 109, 113, 120,
  121
Deliberate Doubt: 72, 73
Despair: 69, 73, 89
Devil (Satan, Lucifer): 3, 7, 35, 56,
  58, 61, 62, 63, 64, 71
Discord: 45, 79
Disobedience: 38, 56, 76
Disrespect: 74, 76

Divorce: 10, 47, 60, 83, 85
Drunkenness: 47, 48, 59, 78, 85, 94
Duties of Our State In Life: 48, 90

E

Egoism: 19, 63
Escrivá, Blessed Josemaría,
    Monsignor Escrivá: 123, 141
Eternity: 1, 2, 3, 14, 18, 26, 33,
    34, 35, 36, 45, 52, 56, 57, 58,
    67, 83, 90, 110, 142
Eucharist (Blessed Sacrament): 17,
    26, 75, 117, 128, 134, 142
Euthanasia: 59, 78, 85
Examination of Conscience
    (general exam, particular
    exam): 67, 104, 105, 106,
    107, 108, 113

F

Fatima: 57
Fornication: 46, 80, 94, 99
Fraud: 48, 60, 80, 99
Freedom: 6, 7, 9, 61, 62, 78, 97,
    98, 99, 118, 122, 138
Freedom of conscience: 98
Frequent Confession: 6, 33, 34,
    49, 86, 93, 94, 95, 123
Fundamental Option Theory:
    60, 61

G

General Absolution: 121, 122
Gifts of the Holy Spirit: 86, 101,
    127, 131, 132
God's will: 6, 64, 129
Gossip: 39, 45, 46, 62, 82, 85,
    106, 109
Grace: 6, 7, 8, 20, 28, 29, 30, 31,
    32, 33, 34, 35, 37, 47, 56, 60,
    61, 64, 72, 86, 94, 101, 117,
    119, 120, 121, 123, 125,
    126,131, 133, 134, 135, 136,
    139, 140, 141
Grace (actual): 126, 132, 133,
    134, 136
Grace (sacramental): 27, 123, 133
Grace (sanctifying): 8, 14, 27, 31,
    53, 56, 93, 101, 123, 125,
    126, 127, 129, 130, 131, 132,
    133, 134, 140
Grave sin: 69, 70, 74, 79, 116

H

Hatred: 32, 39, 45, 58, 73, 78, 129
Hatred of God: 58, 73, 129
Heaven: 2, 5, 14, 15, 16, 21, 31,
    57, 59, 70, 90, 91, 120, 126,
    128, 136
Hell: 1, 31, 33, 52, 56, 57, 58, 94,
    110, 120, 128
Holiness: 11, 19, 38, 74, 103, 116,
    134, 135, 142
Holy Spirit: 27, 54, 61, 80, 86,
    100, 101, 109, 112, 119, 120,
    126, 127, 130, 131, 132, 141
Homosexuality: 46
How Do We Sin (thoughts, desires,
    words, actions, omissions):
    37, 39
How To Make A Good Confes-
    sion: 104
Human Respect: 32, 84
Humility: 28, 42, 67, 83, 87, 107,
    108, 139
Hypocrisy: 41, 42, 63

I

Idolatry: 56, 59, 70, 71
Ignorance: 8, 58, 59, 61, 62, 68,
    69, 72, 97, 98
Ignorance (invincible): 68, 69
Ignorance (vincible): 69
In vitro fertilization: 60
Insults: 45, 79
Intellect: 37, 42, 45, 56, 125, 131,
    140
Irreligion: 19, 70, 71

J

Jealousy: 4, 39, 45, 83, 116
John Paul II: 9, 10, 13, 20, 28, 38,
    39, 40, 52, 59, 68, 79, 96, 99,
    103, 109, 117, 119, 121, 122
Judgment: 39, 41, 45, 69, 82, 95,
    99, 100, 137, 140

L

Lukewarmness: 49, 73
Luxury: 3, 44, 63

M

Magisterium: 38, 67, 68
Mary of Egypt: 19
Mass: 6, 39, 49, 54, 59, 61, 70,
    75, 83, 86, 87, 107, 113, 132,
    133, 134, 135, 136
Masturbation: 46, 60
Materialism: 43, 63, 64, 70, 83
Mercy: 13, 14, 16, 17, 20, 26, 27,
    28, 30, 32, 34, 35, 39, 52, 58,
    60, 67, 69, 73, 75, 78, 84, 85,
    86, 87, 88, 89, 90, 91, 103,
    104, 109, 111, 115, 116, 119,
    120, 126, 128
Miserliness: 44
Moral obligations: 38
Moral teachings of the Catholic
    Church: 29, 31, 38
Morbid curiosity: 44, 45
Mortifications: 113, 114
Murder: 18, 60, 78, 99

N

Natural law: 37, 38, 65, 95, 96,
    99, 100, 136
Natural moral virtues: 130
Necessity Of Sorrow: 109
New Rite of Penance: 119
Niggardliness: 44

O

Oaths: 74
Occult: 45, 71
Ostentation: 41, 42, 63
Our Lady: 51, 57, 74, 75, 116

P

Passions: 19, 41, 54, 56, 64
Penance: 9, 12, 13, 17, 20, 21, 22,
    25, 28, 29, 36, 52, 55, 93,
    103, 104, 108, 109, 110, 111,
    112, 113, 114, 117, 118, 119,
    120, 121, 122, 123, 126

Perjury: 60, 74, 82
Pornography: 46, 60, 80
Prayer: 6, 19, 28, 31, 41, 47, 49,
    54, 70, 73, 76, 77, 83, 86, 87,
    88, 121, 134, 135, 140, 142
Precepts: 67, 69, 83, 84, 100, 109
Preparation For Confession: 109
Presumption: 34, 41, 61, 73, 79
Pride: 19, 30, 41, 42, 43, 45, 49,
    58, 61, 63, 64, 74, 79, 87,
    106, 108, 109
Pride of life: 63
Profanity: 74
Prostitution: 59, 78
Purgatory: 36, 52, 53, 88, 113,
    128
Purpose of life: 5, 22, 94

Q

Quarrels: 41, 45, 59, 79

R

Rape: 46, 60
Rash judgment: 39, 45, 82
Religious indifferentism: 72
Revealing secrets: 45
Revenge: 45
Rosary: 49, 54, 86, 87, 107

S

Sacrilege: 46, 70, 72, 99, 111, 118
Salvation: 27, 28, 36, 61
Sanctification: 108, 126, 133,
    134, 135, 141
Sanctity: 64, 67, 130, 135, 141,
    142
Schism: 72, 73
Scruples: 114, 115, 116
Seal of confession: 30, 112
Selfishness: 61, 63, 79, 84
Sensual appetites: 35
Seton, Elizabeth: 125
Seven Capital Sins: 41, 107
Sex education: 40, 85
Simony: 70, 72
Sin (mortal): 12, 17, 19, 27, 33,
    39, 49, 51, 52, 53, 54, 56, 57,
    58, 59, 60, 61, 69, 71, 72, 73,

74, 75, 84, 111, 112, 118,
126, 129, 130, 133, 139
Sin (original): 41, 82, 104
Sin (personal): 41, 53, 122
Sin (venial): 52, 53, 54, 55, 74,
75, 140
Sister Josefa Menendez: 123
Situation Ethics: 60
Slander: 39, 45, 46, 82
Sloth: 41, 47, 48, 49, 108
Soul: 2, 3, 4, 5, 8, 17, 20, 21, 23,
27, 28, 29, 30, 33, 35, 48, 49,
52, 53, 54, 56, 57, 58, 76, 90,
91, 97, 101, 103, 104, 108,
122, 125, 126, 130, 131, 132
Spiritual sloth: 49, 73
St. Alphonsus Maria De Liguori:
43
St. Thomas Aquinas: 139
St. Augustine: 99
St. Bernard: 34
St. Catherine of Siena:
12, 27, 52, 125
St. Caesarius: 34
St. Gregory: 34, 54
St. Ignatius: 64
St. John: 10, 18, 26, 101, 127
St. Monica: 18
St. Thomas More: 125
St. Paul: 7, 18, 19, 31, 37, 39, 40,
59, 60, 64, 69, 79, 81, 105
St. Peter: 18, 37, 108
St. Peter Julian Eymard: 108
St. Rose of Lima: 84
St. Teresa of Ávila: 41, 52
St. Wilfrid: 101
Sterilization: 78, 96
Suicide: 10, 59, 78, 94
Supernatural virtues: 127
Superstition: 70, 71

T

Talebearing: 45
Temporal punishment: 35, 120
Tempting God: 70, 71
Ten Commandments: 38, 39, 65,

67, 68, 69, 70, 81, 83, 94,
100, 109, 136
The World, The Flesh, And The
Devil: 3, 61
Trust in God: 5, 115, 128

U

Unbelief: 72

V

Vanity: 41, 42, 43, 54, 63, 79
Vasectomy: 60, 78
Vatican II: 28, 118
Venerable Louis of Granada: 34,
35, 54
Vices: 5, 10, 33, 34, 35, 41, 45,
49, 54, 73, 76, 81, 95, 111,
122, 137
Virtues: 39, 41, 49, 70, 77, 94,
107, 108, 115, 123, 127, 129,
130, 131, 132, 137, 138, 139,
140, 141, 142
Virtues (infused moral): 129, 130,
131, 139, 141
Virtues (infused theological):
127, 140
Vows: 74

W

Will: 3, 4, 5, 6, 8, 15, 35, 37, 38,
45, 48, 56, 58, 59, 61, 62, 64,
101, 116, 125, 130, 131, 132,
134, 135, 137, 138, 140
Works of mercy: 34, 67, 69, 75,
84, 85, 109